Mexican Philosophy for the 21st Century

Bloomsbury Introductions to World Philosophies

Series Editor:

Monika Kirloskar-Steinbach

Assistant Series Editor:

Leah Kalmanson

Regional Editors:

Nader El-Bizri, James Madaio, Takeshi Morisato, Pascah Mungwini, Ann A. Pang White, Mickaella Perina, Omar Rivera and Georgina Stewart

Bloomsbury Introductions to World Philosophies delivers primers reflecting exciting new developments in the trajectory of world philosophies. Instead of privileging a single philosophical approach as the basis of comparison, the series provides a platform for diverse philosophical perspectives to accommodate the different dimensions of cross-cultural philosophizing. While introducing thinkers, texts and themes emanating from different world philosophies, each book, in an imaginative and path-breaking way, makes clear how it departs from a conventional treatment of the subject matter.

Titles in the Series:

A Practical Guide to World Philosophies, by Monika Kirloskar-Steinbach and Leah Kalmanson

Daya Krishna and Twentieth-Century Indian Philosophy, by Daniel Raveh

Māori Philosophy, by Georgina Tuari Stewart

Philosophy of Science and the Kyoto School, by Dean Anthony Brink

Tanabe Hajime and the Kyoto School, by Takeshi Morisato

African Philosophy, by Pascah Mungwini

The Philosophy of the Brahma-sūtra, by Aleksandar Uskokov

Sikh Philosophy, by Arvind-Pal Singh Mandair

The Philosophy of the Yogasūtra, by Karen O'Brien-Kop

The Life and Thought of H. Odera Oruka, by Gail M. Presbey

Contextualizing Angela Davis, by Joy James

Mexican Philosophy for the 21st Century

*Relajo, Zozobra, and Other Frameworks
for Understanding Our World*

Carlos Alberto Sánchez

BLOOMSBURY ACADEMIC
LONDON · NEW YORK · OXFORD · NEW DELHI · SYDNEY

BLOOMSBURY ACADEMIC
Bloomsbury Publishing Plc
50 Bedford Square, London, WC1B 3DP, UK
1385 Broadway, New York, NY 10018, USA
29 Earlsfort Terrace, Dublin 2, Ireland

BLOOMSBURY, BLOOMSBURY ACADEMIC and the Diana logo are trademarks
of Bloomsbury Publishing Plc

First published in Great Britain 2023

For legal purposes the Acknowledgments on p. x constitute an extension
of this copyright page.

Series design by Louise Dugdale
Cover image © bgblue / Getty Images

A catalogue record for this book is available from the British Library.

A catalog record for this book is available from the Library of Congress.

ISBN: HB: 978-1-3503-1915-8
PB: 978-1-3503-1914-1
ePDF: 978-1-3503-1916-5
eBook: 978-1-3503-1917-2

Series: Bloomsbury Introductions to World Philosophies

Typeset by Deanta Global Publishing Services, Chennai, India

For Tricia.

Contents

Tables

Series Editor's Preface

The introductions we include in the World Philosophies series take a single thinker, theme, or text and provide a close reading of them. What defines the series is that these are likely to be people or traditions that you have not yet encountered in your study of philosophy. By choosing to include them you broaden your understanding of ideas about the self, knowledge, and the world around us. Each book presents unexplored pathways into the study of world philosophies. Instead of privileging a single philosophical approach as the basis of comparison, each book accommodates the many different dimensions of cross-cultural philosophizing. While the choice of terms used by the individual volumes may indeed carry a local inflection, they encourage critical thinking about philosophical plurality. Each book strikes a balance between locality and globality.

Mexican Philosophy for the 21st Century is a fine illustration of recent philosophical work that departs from conventional survey models of world philosophies. Its author Carlos Alberto Sánchez invites the reader to explore our world by using concepts that have been developed and honed through the Mexican experience. Sánchez carefully guides the reader from an interruption of statis (*relajo*) to an experience of simultaneous convergence and divergence (*nepantla*). Following upon the heels of such a concrete experience of in-betweenness, one would be inclined to test out the faculty of heart-knowing (*corazonadas*) in making meaning of our world of modern uncertainty. Deployed simultaneously by several people, an organic sense of community (*tik*) would develop. This in turn would enable community members to interpret their pictures of the world and adapt them to the feeling of anxiety (*zozobra*) that sets in due to the conflicting demands the world places on us.

—Monika Kirloskar-Steinbach

Acknowledgments

This book is the result of multiple conversations, talks, disagreements, and compromises with many wonderful people for whom Mexican philosophy is a true passion. I'm especially indebted to Robert Sanchez, Manuel Vargas, Clinton Tolley, Amy Oliver, Francisco Gallegos, Guillermo Hurtado, Carlos Pereda, and Aurelia Valero. Drafts of chapters contained in this book were presented (some virtually) in various places, including Boston University's Department of Philosophy, SOAS University of London, Benemérita Universidad Autónoma de Puebla, and Instituto de Investigaciones Filosóficas UNAM—to the attendees, I am especially grateful. I would also like to thank my editor at Bloomsbury, Colleen Coalter, and series editors, Monika Kirloskar and Omar Rivera, for their patience, leadership, and abundance of grace. The anonymous referees were also invaluable. Finally, for their unending moral and spiritual support, I am forever grateful to my wife, Tricia, and my teenage critics, Julian, Ethan, and Pascual.

Introduction

Mexican Philosophy: What It Is and Why It Matters

Not long ago, it would have been inconceivable to suggest that certain of our contemporary human crises would be better served if looked at through the lens of Mexican philosophy. It would have been inconceivable, *especially outside of Mexico*, because the conceptual resources that would make such analyses possible had not yet been sufficiently articulated in English, "philosophy's modern-day *lingua franca*."[1] Today there are translations of primary texts in Mexican philosophy, a growth in the secondary literature, a scholarly journal dedicated to it, and general-audience publications that could facilitate such interventions (see Further Reading). Thus, it is not beyond the realm of conceivability that Mexican philosophy could at any moment be pulled into the fray where different philosophical perspectives are deployed in the service of addressing some of our contemporary catastrophes. However, and despite the availability of resources, and while not inconceivable, the deployment of Mexican philosophy for this purpose would still be *extraordinary*. This extraordinariness points to the situation of Mexican philosophy outside of Mexico: it points to its marginalization and its struggle for legitimacy.

In this introductory chapter, I consider the state of Mexican philosophy *outside of Mexico*.[2] My very general aim is to make a case for the inclusion of Mexican philosophy into the register of global philosophical traditions or "world philosophies."[3] I am motivated by an assumption that seems quite obvious to those of us that work on this tradition, namely, that Mexican philosophy *is not currently* counted among the many philosophical traditions we currently count.[4] I suspect that this lack of inclusion is tied to certain doubts about its legitimacy—that is, it is not thought of as a "real" philosophical tradition.

I link legitimization to what the Argentine philosopher Francisco Romero called "normalization," and propose that while Mexican philosophy has not yet achieved normalization *outside of Mexico* as, say, Chinese or Indian philosophy, both its history and the conceptual resources it offers sufficiently legitimate its inclusion as a tradition worth thinking about. In other words, recognizing that certain concepts and approaches belonging to Mexican philosophy uniquely contribute to a more inclusive and global conception of philosophy and the philosophical reveals its legitimacy and helps *normalize* the notion that certain of our contemporary human crises are better served when looked at through its lenses.

In pushing for Mexican philosophy's inclusion into the global philosophical conversation, it will be necessary to highlight its salient features. These include a commitment to and dependence on circumstance, culture, and history, a unique philosophical vocabulary mined in the Mexican experience and, importantly, a historically informed *anti*-Europeanness. These features, especially the last, seem somewhat counterintuitive, as the European philosophical tradition has obviously influenced the very notion of a Mexican "philosophy." To be clear, however, Mexican philosophy, while *anti*-European, is not non-Western, as it necessarily traffics in Western history; rather, what I mean is that it is "post-Western" in the sense that while a product of Western intervention in the "New World," it does *not* find itself beholden to those criteria that the West has authorized as essential to capital-P "Philosophy"—in its methods, themes, and its vocabulary, it has, intentionally or not, clearly violated the dictates of that tradition.

Mexican philosophy's post-Westernness, moreover, may also explain its struggle for legitimacy or normalcy. It may explain, that is, the "reasons" as to why it continues to exist as a marginal, and even invisible, tradition *outside Mexico*. To this end, I consider the process of normalization and the reasons why Mexican philosophy has not been normalized *outside of Mexico*, particularly in the English-speaking world. Suggesting that entering this process is sufficient or enough to dislodge Mexican philosophy from the periphery, bringing it and its resources to light, I end by proposing that Mexican philosophy as tradition, as well as its figures, methods, and texts, can supplement, enrich, and broaden the scope and depth of our philosophical understanding and our philosophical curriculum.

1. A Post-Western Philosophical Tradition

Mexican philosophy is an accident of history. More specifically, Mexican philosophy is a byproduct of Western philosophy's role in the colonization of the Americas, a role that involved the rationalization, justification, and clarification of the conquest and the subjugation of indigenous peoples along with their ways of knowing. In this role, the philosophy of Aristotle, St. Thomas Aquinas, St. Augustine, and so on, meant to make sense of this "new" world, both for the conquerors and for the conquered. However, this project of "making sense" was not disembodied or merely intellectual.

Western philosophy was placed in the trenches, tasked with forming and instructing non-Western peoples into Western worldviews. There were consequences to this involvement. In the process of erasing and replacing indigenous knowledges (or ways of knowing original to the "new" world), Western philosophy was confiscated by those it sought to form and instruct. Recognizing it as a way to more easily communicate with their conquerors, it was appropriated for ends benefiting the "new" circumstance. Through such "contamination," Western philosophy lost its purity until what remained was but a hybrid, nepantla, philosophy that spoke from its own place and through its own experience about its own urgencies and needs. In the twentieth century, it would call itself "Mexican philosophy."

When scholars of Western philosophical history insist that Mexican philosophy is nothing but Western philosophy by another name, what they miss or ignore are the effects of its confiscation. They are then forced to conclude that Mexican philosophy is but a redundancy and, ultimately, unremarkable. The same with scholars of *non*-Western philosophy for whom Mexican philosophy's relation with the West means that the latter is but a branch of the former's intellectual tree—in this case, Mexican philosophy is not "non-Western" but merely Western philosophy, pure and simple.

My claim is that Mexican philosophy is *not Western* in the sense of being but a branch of the Western philosophical tree, but also that it is *not non-Western* in the sense that it can be considered part of the "non-Western" philosophical tradition (like Indian or Chinese philosophy). I call it "post-Western."

In calling Mexican philosophy post-Western, I signal its post-coloniality. That is, Mexican philosophy is post-Western for the simple reason that in its appropriations of the Western tradition, it seeks to go beyond its own inheritance while being true to its place. The philosopher Emilio Uranga (1949) articulates this idea best when he writes: "[Mexican philosophy] will make its own particular turn toward the universal, appropriating the European without apology, feeling in the European spirit something co-natural but simultaneously capable of being overcome" (241).

In fact, Uranga's own refusal to accept the European notion of "humanity" markedly illustrates Mexican philosophy's post-Westernness. Uranga writes:

> *Any interpretation of the human as a substantial creature seems to us inhuman.* At the origins of our history we suffered a devaluation for failing to assimilate ourselves to European "humanity." In a similar spirit, today we reject that qualification and, thus, refuse to recognize as "human" any European construction that grounds human "dignity" in substantiality. (Uranga 2021, 109)

With Uranga's rejection of "that qualification," one involving a notion of humanity fully in line with European ideals about culture, race, faith, and so on,[5] Mexican philosophy takes a stand *against* the ideological currents of Western philosophy and returns to itself as the proper adjudicating source of "dignity" and what it means to be human. This poses a challenge to the "arrogance" of the Western tradition (see Chapter 6). In challenging Western arrogance in this way, Mexican philosophy positions itself as post-Western, which also means that *it is both not Western but also not non-Western* (i.e., it is not specifically devoid of a Western influence, e.g., Aztec philosophy). In its indeterminacy, Mexican philosophy is "nepantla."

What does this mean? By virtue of its character of indeterminacy—of neither this nor that, I consider Mexican philosophy as a "neptantla" philosophical tradition ("nepantla" is the subject of Chapter 3), which means that it occupies a philosophical and historical no-man's land, a middle ground and *in-betweenness*, one where it moves across *multiple philosophical orientations* that both nourish and reject it as simultaneously familiar and alien to themselves. The consequences of this rejection are a silencing, denial, and marginalization that helps account for Mexican philosophy's lack of recognition as a real philosophical option, especially *outside* of Mexico.

Recognition comes with normalization. What does normalization mean for Mexican philosophy? Normalization means, at the very least, that teaching it, writing about it, or promoting it in various ways will not be a risky practice; that one can still get tenure, promotion, and book contracts; moreover, that seeing it appear on conference programs or journal table of contents will not be cause for panic. For those of us currently working in this tradition, however, normalization also means that it is recognized as a significant contribution to the history of philosophy, understood generally as humanity's historical love affair with wisdom. In any event, this is why *I* seek its normalization.

Some will counter that by normalization I actually mean something like approval or authorization by the philosophical establishment, something that would require a levelling or an erasure of whatever makes it different. And this is bad. After all, does not the marginality, nepantla, or post-Westernness of Mexican philosophy reflect a certain modern sensibility for heterogeneity and difference, one that gives it an edge that general acceptance would nullify? More damning still: Could my desire for the normalization of Mexican philosophy simply be the manifestation of a deep-seated colonial anxiety about not being taken seriously myself?

My call for normalization is not about a levelling whereby Mexican philosophy can thereby measure up to established, Western, standards of what philosophy should be or what it should deal with. Rather, normalization is intimately related to more concrete concerns, namely, to contemporary demands for counterhegemonic philosophical interventions, multicultural representation in our syllabi, and inclusivity in our faculty. Moreover, normalcy is not a process of erasure whereby a philosophical tradition must relinquish its difference; it is a process of recognition, whereby that difference is allowed to participate in an ongoing, and global, philosophical drama.

2. A Definition

Mexican philosophy is "Mexican" in the straightforward sense that in its origins it is a reflection on Mexican reality, identity, and culture. In the twentieth century,[6] it sought to clarify the nature of Mexicanness, Mexican being, or what it meant to be Mexican (what philosophers called "lo mexicano"). In a more complicated sense, the "Mexican" in Mexican philosophy is meant to indicate its non-Europeanness, insisting, as Leopoldo Zea (2017) does, that "[o]ur situation is not that of the European bourgeoisie. Our philosophy, if it is to be responsible, does not make the same commitments that contemporary European philosophy does" (137). However, in framing itself as non-European it will not deny the European influence; colonialism has made this influence unavoidable. But in calling itself "Mexican" it means to confront it, to process it, to metabolize it, and thus to arrive at its own, postcolonial, post-Western identity. This means that while we can think of Mexican philosophy figuratively as a branch of Western philosophy's family tree, it is a branch that, in neglect, has broken off, fallen to the ground, and now lays partly in its shadow, partly in the sun.

In being partly in and partly out, Mexican philosophy is hard to characterize. Again, it is obviously not non-Western like Africana, Islamic, Chinese, or Indian philosophy. However, it is also *not* non-Western like pre-Columbian philosophy, to which it is at least historically related.[7] That it resists these categorizations, however, does not mean that it should just be avoided. Its value lies precisely in its indeterminateness, in its *nepantla*.

We know what Mexican philosophy is *not*. We are now in a position to say what Mexican philosophy *is*. To this end, I offer two versions of a "working definition," both of which are merely tentative approximations, open to revision, rejection, and reconsideration.

Version 1: "Mexican philosophy" refers to a nepantla philosophical tradition (neither Western nor non-Western, but in between) that values: (a) the formative or constitutive influence of history and circumstance, (b) cultural or spiritual particularity or difference, and (c), the epistemic priority of lived experience.[8]

Version 2: Mexican philosophy orients us to the immediacy of our circumstantial reality with concepts and methods that while gathered via reflections on the Mexican experience, tend toward a kind of inclusivity that embraces a multitude of experiences, crises, and catastrophes, including, but especially, those of peoples at the periphery, the bottom (*los de abajo*), and the outside.

Either of these, version 1 or 2, is already a much broader, expansive, and inclusive definition of Mexican philosophy than what has been previously proposed, namely, as "a philosophy that reflects from Mexico and says something to Mexico" (Hurtado 2007, 10).[9] Or similarly, as a tradition about Mexicans and for Mexicans. In both of the current versions, this definition captures at least two of Mexican philosophy's most salient features: first, place, as both as an epistemological and ontological priority, and second, difference as a hermeneutical starting point.

The question becomes how Mexican philosophy is any different than other philosophical traditions given that *place* and *difference* are likewise characteristic of other traditions or approaches. My hope is that this book answers this question. For now, we can say that Mexican philosophers appeal to a sort of intuition (or "corazonada," this will be the theme of Chapter 4) that reveals a "character" or an "atmosphere" that differentiates it and which belongs only to Mexican philosophy when encountered in the reading of its texts or the thinking of its concepts. Jorge Portilla (2012) describes the experience as follows:

> Just as the structures of the self are not reachable by direct intuition, it is probable that the essential structures of a national spirit are not either . . . with stolen glances and out of the corner of my eye . . . a character is accessible to me only . . . I cannot see "Frenchness" in a pure state as I see these trees on the other side of the street, but I can see it sideways, as a style, as an atmosphere that is not directly graspable, found in the characters and actions of a novel, in the treatise on civil war, or in the work of a philosopher. (127–8)

What these "stolen glances" reveal allow us to scaffold our definition earlier, both versions of which communicate a similar phenomenon and both of which can be easily taught.

3. Characteristics: Place or Circumstance

According to Leopoldo Zea (1912–2004), Samuel Ramos' *Profile of Man and Culture in Mexico*, published in 1934, signals the arrival of Mexican philosophy by elevating "Mexican culture as theme for philosophical interpretation" (1942, 63). Zea, a younger contemporary of Ramos, proclaims that with *Profile of Man* "philosophy descends from the world of ideal entities and toward the world of concrete entities such as Mexico, itself a symbol of men and women that live and die in its cities and in its mountains" (63). We can call this a "humbling" of (Western) philosophy, and it makes possible the emergence of a concrete Mexican philosophy. On earth, among the living and the dying, philosophy is given a new task, one demanded by concreteness itself. The task: "to go to the history of [Mexican] culture and extricate from it themes for a new philosophical preoccupation" (63).

Of course, capital-P Philosophy will resist the *humbling*, what it interprets as *humiliation*. Debates will ensue about whether or not such a terrestrial philosophizing meets the Authoritative Standard of Philosophy—a Standard that demands that Philosophy remain immune to the urgencies of place, time, and biography so that it may unbiasedly pursue the sort of unqualified universality that applies to all, at all times, and in all places. Leaning on the standard, critics of Zea's "circumstantialism"[10] will relegate his "humble" approach to the realms of nonphilosophy, for instance, to cultural or ethnic studies, literature, poetry, or, when generous, intellectual history. In Latin America more generally, the resistance comes from those who argue that in order to have a genuine Latin American philosophy, and by extension, a Mexican philosophy, there first needs to be a genuine Latin American/Mexican culture—an impossibility, so long as colonialism is still operative in Latin America (see, especially, Bondy 1968). For Zea, however, this is not a problem, because the possibility of a genuine culture appears as a first philosophical problem, and a genuine Latin American philosophical problem at that, thereby lending credence to the notion that Latin American philosophy *is philosophy*.

> In posing and trying to solve the problem [as to whether or not there is a genuine culture], independently of whether or not the answer is in the affirmative or not, is to already do [Mexican] philosophy since it tries to answer, in an affirmative or negative way, a question belonging to [Mexico]. (Zea 1942, 64)

Moreover,

> It is worth asking ourselves why it is that we cannot have a philosophy proper to ourselves, and the answer perhaps will be a philosophy proper to ourselves. (74)

Philosophy is thus understood as a grappling with questions that arise from the necessity to understand one's concrete existence or circumstance. Mexican philosophy is possible and original when it does this. Zea continues:

> [W]e have a series of problems that are only given in our circumstance . . . that can only be resolved by us. The positing of such problems will not diminish the philosophical character of our philosophy, because philosophy tries to resolve problems posed to one in one's existence. The problems posed . . . will have to be specific to circumstance where one lives. (73)

This commitment to place, what here and elsewhere I call "circumstantialism," is central to Mexican philosophy.

The Mexican circumstance (in Ortega y Gasset's (2000) sense of *Circum stantia*—"the mute things which stand all around us" (41)) necessarily includes the social and political reality of Mexico, the plight of its people, but especially its history—a history shaped by conquest, colonization, and imperialism, old and new. Less abstractly, however, the circumstance is the *space* and *time* that informs Mexican identity, allowing each person to *make sense* of the world from *that* particular place and given *that* particular history. Reflection on that circumstance constitutes the starting point for Mexican philosophy as defined in version 1 and 2 earlier (from this starting point, however, one can likewise speak to more general concerns which are less bounded and less determined by them). Thus, I insist, with Guillermo Hurtado (2007), that "[f]or Mexican philosophy to truly be Mexican it must take a reflection on its reality as its point of departure, or it must originate in it" (42).

4. The Issue of Normalization

The Argentine philosopher Francisco Romero (1943) divided the history of philosophy in Latin America into three periods: the period of founding when philosophy began to be taken seriously; the period of normalization, wherein philosophy became an accepted academic discipline—this is a period of settling and expanding; and the period of modernization, when Latin American philosophers could be said to have contributed to the philosophical conversation, in their own language, in significant ways.[11] Our concern here is with the second period. Romero notes that during a period of "normalcy" one finds that "more measured and more methodological work is everywhere undertaken" resulting in conference presentations, articles, and books which showcase a general love for philosophy, but also originality, distinctiveness, and daring in philosophical approaches (131). During this period, it is common for philosophy to enter the public sphere where it can be discussed, scrutinized, nurtured, or rejected.

Zea adopts Romero's periodization and suggests that Mexican philosophers have indeed entered a period of normalization—of settling and expansion—by the early 1940s. At this time, there is a surge in philosophical publications, "as well as the formation of institutes and centers for philosophical studies" (Zea 1942, 63). Thus, Zea suggests that philosophy, in Mexico in particular, but in Latin America more generally, has entered a

> stage of philosophical normalcy . . . a stage in which the exercise of philosophy is seen as an ordinary function of culture in the same way as other activities of a cultural nature. The philosopher is no longer seen as an extravagant that no one understands and comes to be a member of the culture of her country. A *"philosophical climate"* establishes itself. (63)

As we use it here, the concept of normalization barrows from both Romero and Zea and has two senses: the first sense refers to the normalization of philosophy in a determinate society or culture; the second sense refers to the normalization of a particular philosophical tradition in a culture in which philosophy itself is already normalized.[12] It is in the second sense of normalization that I have in mind when I talk about the normalization of Mexican philosophy *outside of Mexico*.

We can summarize normalization in the first sense as follows:

(1a) An acceptance of philosophy in the culture;

(1b) An understanding of methodological commitments to
philosophical approaches;

(1c) Dissemination of philosophical production via publications,
conferences, and institutes.

To these, we add:

(1d) A conceptual archive.

These characteristics of normalization in turn point to:

(1e) The establishment of a "philosophical climate" in which
philosophy can flourish.

The presence of these characteristics means that philosophy as a
practice and field of study, as something to which people may dedicate
themselves in personal and professional ways, is not extraordinary, but
common or normal. The established "climate" allows it and promotes it.

Normalization in the second sense refers to the normalization of a
specific philosophical tradition in places where philosophy itself has
already achieved normalization. In the second sense, the characteristics
of normalization are:

(2a) An acceptance of that particular philosophical tradition/
orientation in the culture;

(2b) An understanding of that tradition's methodological
commitments;

(2c) Its dissemination via publications, conferences, and institutes;

(2d) The identification of a conceptual archive belonging to it.

These, in turn, point to:

(2e) the existence of a "philosophical climate" in which that tradition
is no longer ignored, marginalized, or rejected.

Mexican philosophy *in Mexico* enters a period of normalcy in the *first sense*
in the late 1940s as a new generation adopts and deploys phenomenology,
existentialism, and historicism in order to grapple with the problem of

Mexican identity—a project also known as "la filosofía de lo mexicano" (see Villegas 1979; Hurtado 2006; Sánchez 2016).[13] Nourished by the climate of philosophical acceptance in Latin America as a whole (1e), the "filosofía de lo mexicano" achieves normalcy in the first sense for a short period of time, before its overcoming by more *traditional* philosophical methodologies (namely, those of analytic philosophy and Marxist critical social theory, in particular). Mexican philosophers contribute widely to these traditions, and hence to philosophy itself, entering in this way a period of philosophical maturity (again, in the first sense). In Mexico, however, maturity leads to the almost total westernization of philosophy, to what Guillermo Hurtado calls "modernization"—a period where Mexican philosophers shed the "Mexican" label and commit to a philosophizing more in line with the universalizing pretentions of European and North American philosophy (Hurtado 2007). This period of maturity/modernization, however, sought to "cannibalize"[14] the previous period where *la filosofía de lo mexicano* had achieved normalcy, where Mexican philosophy *as* Mexican philosophy had found a footing. Today, Mexican philosophy *in Mexico*, as understood during its brief period of normalization, is making a return, although it is not yet normalized as it was in the middle of the twentieth century.

Our concern, however, is not with Mexican philosophy *in Mexico*, thus, in the first sense, but rather with Mexican philosophy as it is written, read, and taught *outside* of Mexico, thus with normalization in the second sense. Outside of Mexico, and especially in the United States, we find Mexican philosophy exiting its "founding" period and entering a process of normalization, one that *should* place it on pace for settling and expansion. The problem, however, as we will see in the next section, is that normalization seems difficult for reasons external to philosophy itself.

5. Obstacles to Normalization

What stands in the way of Mexican philosophy's normalization in the second sense? More specifically, what could account for Mexican philosophy's marginalization as a philosophical tradition outside of Mexico? One possible cause is a widespread unfamiliarity with the tradition and consequent unfamiliarity with the conceptual resources or methodologies it avails, some of which can supplement, even enrich, existing metaphysical, epistemological, or ontological accounts of human existence. However, it's one thing to marginalize a philosophical tradition or figure due unfamiliarity; it is another thing entirely to marginalize these because of reasons foreign to philosophy itself.

We can point to at least three reasons that perpetuate the continual marginalization, or non-normalization, of Mexican philosophy outside of Mexico: (1) implicit bias; (2) a resistance to the notion that philosophy can be, in any way, "Mexican"; and (3) the assumption that due to colonial relations, Mexican philosophy is merely a bad imitation of European philosophy.

1. Implicit bias interferes with the normalization of Mexican philosophy in a very straightforward way: the assumption is that due to its history, geopolitical situation, and economic status, Mexico is not capable of producing philosophers, much less philosophy, comparable to those of more developed, industrialized, "first world" countries.[15] Based on this assumption, Mexican philosophers, when they make themselves known, are expected to be preoccupied solely with social and political issues—Enrique Dussel, Leopoldo Zea, and Luis Villoro are examples. The assumption is that other kinds of philosophers or philosophies fall outside the scope of the nation's intellectual desires or capabilities.

2. Doubt that philosophy can be, in any way, "Mexican" is a product of the view that philosophy is universal, a-temporal, and unbounded by nation, culture, ethnicity, language, or any other identifier. There are certainly many in the philosophical establishment that hold this view—again, if only implicitly. Jorge Gracia, for instance, one of the most significant advocates for Latin American philosophy in the United States in the second

part of the last century, saw it necessary to develop a new category for such philosophical approaches, calling it "ethnic philosophy." Ethnic philosophies would be those that insist on identifying themselves in this, very *specific*, way, thus reserving the name "philosophy" to those approaches not encumbered by circumstance, history, or identity (Gracia 2003). This, I believe, flows from an ideological commitment to philosophy rooted in the belief that philosophy must be a "view from nowhere." Because a *Mexican* philosophy is, by default, a "view from somewhere," then it cannot be simply "philosophy."

3. Mexican philosophy is just an unoriginal imitation of European philosophy, a repetition of a tradition brought in by conquerors and colonizers, and taught as a means to perpetuate the colony and justify the conquest. As we saw previously, this is partly true. Mexican philosophy is a byproduct of that history. This is a familiar critique also leveled against the possibility of a Latin American philosophy. Famously, the Peruvian philosopher Augusto Salazar Bondy (1925–74) suggested that the reality of colonialism, imperialism, and other capitalist intrusions into Latin America throughout its history have made it impossible for there to be anything like a "unique" or "genuine" Latin American thought. Any philosophy that has arisen in Latin America, he argues, is simply an echo or imitation of Europe. So long as those colonial and imperialistic relations exist, Latin American philosophy will continue to be but a bad imitation of European philosophy (Bondy 1968). Bondy writes that in the archive of Latin American philosophy there is a "correlative absence of original contributions, ideas and theses capable of being incorporated into the tradition of world thought. There is no . . . doctrine with significance and influence on the whole of universal thought" (39). Naturally (and logically), Bondy's critique can be extended to Mexican philosophy. The critique will say that while philosophy has no doubt been practiced in Mexico, and that there have been Mexican philosophers, Mexico's colonial

inheritance prevents it from articulating ideas and theses "capable of being incorporated into the tradition of world thought," thus it is inauthentic to proclaim that there is a genuine or original, Mexican philosophy.

These are only three possible reasons. There may be many more. My point here is simply to touch on what, I believe, contributes to the marginalization of Mexican philosophy, grounding the challenges that this book takes up. Moreover, and while this list is not exhaustive, it indicates the existence of reasons for *not* attending to Mexican philosophy *outside* of Mexico.

Of course, we can challenge and overcome these "reasons" one by one. The first, by continuing the work of exposure; by exposing this tradition to the world outside of Mexico. The second, by highlighting its difference, one tied to Mexican philosophy's post-Western, or nepantla character as this is reflected in its anti-universalizing commitments and its focus on its own concrete, immediate, social, and cultural realities. And the third, by insisting that the very act of trying to capture one's reality with philosophical concepts, whether these concepts are organic to one's reality or not, is already an authentic philosophical act; that while one's thinking may be clouded by a thick colonial fog, by seeking answers to questions that matter to one's existence one is already philosophizing, in spite of the fog.

The skepticism motivating the third point earlier is one that doubts that an "original" philosophy can ever come out of Mexico. Zea and Uranga, for instance, both respond to this by proposing that "originality," in the sense of novelty, is not what matters; that what matters is originality in the sense of *origin*, so that when one articulates one's difference, even if and when it comes out in the language of Western philosophy, it will still be *original* (Zea 1942; Uranga 2021).

Now, is all of this enough to convince philosophy professors to assign readings in Mexican philosophy or enough to lure graduate students to write theses and dissertations on themes, figures, or problems in this tradition? Is addressing these misconceptions enough to convince the average person that philosophy can be "Mexican," just as it can be Chinese, French, or Indian? I am certain that this is a good start. In addition, and at the very least, we can introduce it and spend time with some of its texts in our philosophy classes; requiring more effort, but equally as valuable, we can insert readings into our syllabi, making these inclusive of *all* traditions and reflective of the growing multiculturalism in our departments and in the global philosophical community.

6. For Our Syllabi

Mexican philosophy, as I define it here, has entered a period of normalization *outside of Mexico* in accordance with the second sense of normalization suggested earlier (2a–2e)—particularly in the United States. As I see it, it finds itself in an evolving process (represented by Δ) with the following characteristics:

(3aΔ) There is a *vague recognition* of Mexican philosophy in the culture;

(3bΔ) There is a *partial understanding* of its methodological commitments;

(3cΔ) There is a *growing list* of publications, conferences, and institutes;

(3dΔ) There is an *ongoing* identification of a conceptual archive belonging to it.

These characteristics show it to be on the way to normalization, which means that it will continue to be marginalized and face questions of legitimacy until we get to (2e), the *forming* of a "philosophical climate," in which it will no longer be merely a broken branch of Western philosophy's family tree, but considered in its difference as a valid and significant contribution to philosophy understood in a global, or international, sense. Getting there (to 2e), however, requires more than recognition, understanding, a list of concepts, or a growing bibliography. Establishing a philosophical climate, where intervening on our catastrophes with Mexican philosophy is normalized, requires teaching and exposing it to others; it requires the kind of practical action that readers of this book will recognize.

We are called to make the case that Mexican philosophy is worth reading and worth studying by showing, in part, how it could benefit our current ways of understanding our world. Or, at least, our current ways of understanding philosophy in a more inclusive, global, or international sense. We could achieve this by focusing on 4d∆ and highlighting the concepts already available to us.

For the sake of illustration, consider a typical syllabus for an "Existentialism" course. This typical course will follow a standard script and lean heavily Eurocentric. As the following chart shows, in that course a unit on "existential anxiety" would spend some time on Heidegger and Sartre, probably bookend that with Kierkegaard and Camus, and stop there. A more inclusive, global, syllabus, one at the very least sensitive to the existence of the Mexican philosophical tradition, would include "zozobra" and the work of Emilio Uranga in this same unit (Table 0.1).

Similarly, other syllabi on other topics can also benefit from availing Mexican philosophy's resources to a global audience: for instance, in a course on hermeneutics we can include Luis Villoro's notion of "*figura del mundo*," which refers to that set of basic beliefs that limit our understanding of difference, and at which Villoro arrives while reflecting on the impoverished interpretative frameworks that contributed to the dehumanization of the indigenous peoples of Mexico during the period of colonization (Chapter 6); to a course on epistemology we can likewise add Uranga's notion of "corazonada," which is a knowing which is affective and embodied (Chapter 4); and to a political or social philosophy course, we can add the indigenous notion of "tik," a concept native to the Tojolab'al indigenous community of southern Mexico and which refers to a radical notion of community, or we-ness, where the I, or subjectivity, is a non-functional term (Chapter 5), and so on.

In this and other ways, our courses are better served with the inclusion of Mexican philosophy as a post-Western orientation. We must confront its marginalization and questions about its legitimacy,

Table 0.1. Sample Syllabus Content for Existentialism Course © Carlos Alberto Sánchez

Syllabus Unit	Eurocentric Focus	From Mexican Philosophy
Anxiety	Themes of Anxiety, Angst, Nausea, and so on	Zozobra
Existence	Themes: Being, Becoming, Being-in-the-world; figures such as Sartre, Camus, de Beauvoir, and so on	Nepantla; Emilio Uranga, Elsa Frost, Rosario Castellanos
Interpretation	Themes: hermeneutic circle, interpretive communities; figures: Augustine, Hans-Georg Gadamer, Paul Ricoeur	Figure of the world, arrogant reason; Luis Villoro, Carlos Pereda
Subjectivity	The crowd, the mass; Kierkegaard	Relajo; Portilla
Individualism and Community	Individualism, Perspectivism	Tik, circumstantialism, contemporary indigenous philosophies; Villoro, Portilla, Lenkensdorf
Traditions	French existentialism, German existentialism	Mexistentialism

issues rooted in ideological and structural obstacles that together with the nepantla nature of Mexican philosophy make it hard to decide how exactly to approach it, think about it, and teach it. For now, and with what there is we are exposed to core concepts in Mexican philosophy, or to ways in which Mexican philosophy invites us to engage our world in a more direct way, which are sufficiently robust and complex to at least diversify, if not enrich and broaden, our syllabi.

7. Mexican Philosophy *Inside* and *Outside* Mexico

Throughout this Introduction, I've referred to Mexican philosophy *outside of Mexico*. Why insist on a distinction between *inside* and *outside*? The answer to this question is due, in part, to a phenomenon perceived by Mexican philosophers themselves, namely, that there is, in actuality, Mexican philosophy *inside* and *outside* Mexico. So far, I have held on to the inside-outside distinction strictly as a means to respect the Mexican experience of that phenomenon. However, because the central aim of this book is to show that Mexican philosophy is not just for or about Mexico I must abandon the inside-outside distinction. Although I will no longer employ that distinction, it is nonetheless instructive to consider the *motivations* for the split.

Now, the phenomenon in question manifests itself as the experience, one had by Mexican philosophers, of the way Mexican philosophy is read and interpreted by those of us *outside* of Mexico. What they see is this: as we work to normalize or legitimize Mexican philosophy in places where it is not yet normalized, for instance, in the United States, *our* tendency is to read it through a global lens. As I highlight in the definition given at the outset, Mexican philosophy *while born from a reflection on Mexican reality, lends itself to reflections into a multitude of experiences, crises, and catastrophes, including, but especially, those of peoples forgotten by the center, those who stand at the periphery and the outside.* Thus we deploy Mexican philosophy *outside Mexico* to make sense of many contemporary issues, especially those having to do with experiences with which it has previously dealt but which arise in *our own* circumstances. Thinking of Mexican philosophy in this way is thus to think of it as a global philosophical tradition.

We are thus seen as *reinterpreting* Mexican philosophy in this more inclusive, global, way, resisting the urge to imbue it with the sort of universality that would cover all experiences and all peoples at all times; we believe that this sort of arrogance is reserved for the European philosophical tradition (see Chapter 6).[16] Because it is neither Western nor non-Western, that is, because it is nepantla, it is uncommitted to any one hegemonic vision of the way philosophy ought to be or how it ought to be practiced. By "global," we ultimately mean capable of adaptation to and adoption in other parts of the world.

The phenomenon experienced by Mexican philosophers is perfectly articulated by the Mexican philosopher Guillermo Hurtado.

Published in *La Razón*, an online news and opinion magazine, Hurtado (2021) suggests that the category "Mexican philosophy" is a recent invention. That is, the growing published archive of *filosofía mexicana* in English translation has created the category "Mexican philosophy." This category begins to show up in books, journal articles, conference proceedings, and so on, and involves not just Mexican philosophers talking about a "national philosophy," but an international group of scholars interested in all aspects of the tradition. "National philosophies are no longer castles surrounded by walls. Today each national philosophy is immersed in an interchange, a communication, a transaction" (Hurtado 2021). In this context, we can "today speak of a Mexican Philosophy, understood as a category of an international philosophy" (Ibid.). Hurtado imagines Mexican philosophy, as written and thought about in English, to be of a distinct character from Mexican philosophy, as written and thought about in Spanish (as *filosofía mexicana*). While Hurtado does not specify what else about Mexican philosophy, as written in English, is distinct, the salient difference one can pick out is that it has crossed or transcended Mexico's national borders, and hence, can now be deployed in the service of other concerns or other circumstances. Ultimately, even *filosofía mexicana* will have to reckon with Mexican philosophy as its other.

Thus, to speak of "Mexican philosophy" is to speak of "Mexican philosophy *outside of Mexico*," or "Mexican philosophy in the US," which refers to a more international, immigrant, philosophical tradition that is at once *filosofía mexicana* and also distinct from it due to the manner of its appropriation and the experiential positionality of its practitioners. It is this tradition that I am referring to when I speak of "Mexican philosophy." It is this tradition that is not normalized *in the second sense*, sitting uncomfortably on the periphery, on the fringes, marginalized in academic philosophy both as a tradition and a field of study; it is this tradition which is ignored by both Western and non-Western philosophers; it is this tradition which is *nepantla*.

Tied to its growing archive outside Mexico, that is, to its "internationalization," or globalization, Mexican philosophy must now contend with what it means for it to be "Mexican philosophy" and not merely *filosofía mexicana*. Again, this distinction holds that Mexican philosophy and *filosofía mexicana* are not identical. Hurtado (2021) writes: "The category of Mexican Philosophy allows us to conceive the conformation of a new hybrid philosophy, partly Mexican and partly American, of a theoretical practice that draws on the two traditions and has one foot in each of them." This is Mexican philosophy breaking out of preestablished confines and adapting itself to circumstances that are not Mexican. Hurtado has in mind the work that we do here in the United States to understand, interpret, and teach Mexican philosophy, and the way in which *we* read it through our own lens, our own interpretive frameworks, and our own life experiences as non-Mexican Mexicans, but Americans or Mexican Americans.[17] The idea is that *filtered through* the "American" experience, *filosofía mexicana* reveals something of that experience and, in the process, becomes something else, what Hurtado properly recognizes as "Mexican philosophy."

The "phenomenon" thus appears most clearly as subtle transformation of *filosofía mexicana* into Mexican philosophy. It is a transformation that is experienced and felt and so is sure to have existential consequences for Mexican philosophers themselves, who are forced to reckon with the sudden perceived distancing of their own tradition:

> What consequences will the category of Mexican Philosophy have on filosofía mexicana? . . . Will Mexican Philosophy help *filosofía mexicana* gain new strength as it is reflected in the glossy exteriors of universities on the other side of the border? Does the category of Mexican Philosophy allow us to imagine the formation of a new bilingual and binational discipline? (Hurtado 2021)

The suggestion here is that Mexican philosophy as a "category" captures the sort of hybridity produced in reading *filosofía mexicana* in *another language*. For example, we can imagine reading Jorge

Portilla's reflections on *relajo* and the suspension of seriousness not only as a phenomenon specific to 1950s Mexico but as a phenomenon whose description explains and accounts for behaviors and attitudes in our own social and historical context, applicable to our lives, and both connected and disconnected from its origin (Chapter 1). In this case, one has deployed both Mexican philosophy and the concept of "relajo" to make sense of our immediate experience and in so doing hybridized the concept of relajo and internationalized Portilla. Hurtado asks what the consequences of this will be, if any. He envisions a renaissance in *filosofía mexicana*, an awakening to its potential, carried out by philosophers in Mexico motivated by those outside Mexico; he also envisions a refocusing on original texts, a return to the origins of Mexican philosophy in Spanish driven by the desire for accuracy in translation or interpretation; and he envisions the creation of an inter-American, bilingual, philosophical conversation that will finally dislodge Mexican philosophy from the peripheries of the global philosophical conversation. Lofty but realizable goals for a *normalized* Mexican philosophy. He thus asks Mexican philosophers in Mexico to consider rethinking their dogmas:

> Perhaps it is time that we left behind two old dogmas of our culture: that of Mexican philosophy can only be done within the borders of Mexico and that Mexican philosophy can only be done in the Spanish language . . . let's not forget that Mexican philosophy has been written in several languages: it was written in Latin [during the colonial period], it has always been written in the original languages of the territory, such as Nahuatl, and now there is also in English [in the United States]. (Hurtado 2021)

In spite of the differences, Hurtado does not seek to divorce Mexican philosophy from *filosofía mexicana*. His provocations are merely an attempt to seduce Mexican philosophers into taking their own tradition more seriously. We could imagine that once Mexican philosophy—as a more global philosophical tradition—crosses the border back into Mexico, Mexican philosophers won't help but find in it the "alienated majesty" of certain thoughts that Emerson (1993) suggests come back to haunt us when we fail to appreciate our own genius (19).

∗   ∗   ∗

So I think Hurtado is right, and it is time to get rid of the "two old dogmas" of Mexican philosophy, which also means ridding ourselves of the inside-outside distinction for good and speak from now on of Mexican philosophy without such qualifications.

Thought as a philosophical tradition that can be deployed globally, I thus propose the following characteristics for a normalized Mexican philosophy in the second sense discussed earlier, some of which are addendums to its definition (Versions 1 and 2 in Section 1):

(i)   It is *written* for an international audience;
(ii) It is *filtered* through a non-Mexican experience;
(iii) It is *demanded by the reality* of multiculturalism and/or, alternatively, by the hegemony of Euro-Western philosophical models and approaches;
(iv) It values *difference*, heterogeneity, and hybridity of all kinds;
(v)   It is proposed as a *nepantla philosophical tradition*, that is, as committed neither to Western philosophical orthodoxy nor to any other established tradition;
(vi) It is deployed in the service of *our* concerns (where "our" is all-inclusive).

Again, this list is not exhaustive. I set it here as a provocation and an exhortation, namely, to think from, about, or after Mexican philosophy.

When we speak of Mexican philosophy, we thus refer to a twentieth and twenty-first-century tradition with its own distinctive approaches, concepts, and figures which are "Mexican" in the sense that they are historically anchored to considerations of the Mexican circumstance but have not remained there. In thinking with and about these approaches, concepts, and figures we grapple with Mexican philosophy and learn from it.

In the long run, there is a global scope to the project of making the case for Mexican philosophy, one framed by the idea that what Mexican philosophy contributes to our contemporary world is a conceptual archive as well as various methodologies which themselves offer ways to approach and engage plurivalent, postcolonial, and contemporary realities by taking seriously the formative and grounding nature of circumstance, identity, and difference, a project that makes *thinking* about its normalization a critical project of philosophical decolonization.

8. The Plan of This Book

There is, among Mexican philosophers, an effort to prioritize what Western philosophy has deprioritized. Perhaps due to its post-Westernness, Mexican philosophy seeks to promote what has been previously demoted, to affirm what has been denied, and to lend a voice to what has been silenced. We see this in the concepts and themes that Mexican philosophers chose to champion, and with which I will be preoccupied for the remainder of this book: relajo, zozobra, nepantla, and corazonada. Of course, this doesn't mean that Mexican philosophers will shy away from other more traditionally philosophical themes. Hence, in what follows, I will also consider the arrogance of reason, inclusive notions of community, and existentialism *a la* Mexicana (Mexistentialism). When these more traditional philosophical themes are treated, they will nonetheless retain some of their "local color," to use a phrase of Jorge Portilla's, and we will see in that treatment the unique difference that Mexican philosophy represents.

The following chapters present those concepts in Mexican philosophy that can help us make better sense of our world or, at the very least, diversify our conceptual arsenal in our efforts to make better sense of it. In Chapter 1, I consider the concept of **relajo**. My claim is that relajo captures a particular social phenomenon where one finds oneself "caught up" in acts of value-inversion or value destruction; in short, relajo is the suspension of seriousness. In Chapter 2, I consider the concept of **nepantla**. Nepantla describes a being in-between, that is, a being in the middle of things. I make the claim that nepantla describes the being of persons who are constantly in the process of finding their way, always en route, and never settled. Related to nepantla, in Chapter 3 I treat the concept of **zozobra**. Zozobra names the anxiety of not knowing where one stands at any one time, the feeling of sinking and drowning that overtakes one in moments of despair or in times of catastrophe, or the feeling of being pulled from all sides by conflicting demands.

Moving to questions of knowledge, Chapter 4 discusses and reflects on Uranga's notion of "ontological intimation," or **corazonada**. An "ontologoical corazonada" or "ontological intimation" refers to an experience of certainty rooted in the immediacy of an emotional/affective encounter/immersion with or in a determinate or familiar state of affairs.

In Chapter 5, I discuss the idea of community as radical inclusivity. The thrust of this chapter is the indigenous notion of **tik**, or "we-ness." Tik refers to a radical conception of community as an inclusive, participatory, plurality where the priority of the individual is displaced in favor of the needs, wants, and care of the other. Tik is an indigenous concept describing the community as an organic and radical we-ness (*grupo nostrico*).

While not necessarily confined to Mexican philosophy, I then reflect on the hermeneutical notion of "**figure of the world**" in Chapter 6. The "figure of the world" is the basic interpretive framework belonging to any culture or peoples that delimits its experience and circumscribe what it allows to make sense. The "Western" figure of the world explains the tendency to dehumanize, objectify, or marginalize other-than-Anglo Europeans. It applies to any use of reason, knowledge, or understanding that takes itself as the standard measure for all others.

Finally, Chapter 7 deals with a concept that is not found in Mexican philosophy but is definitely suggested by my readings of this tradition, what I call **Mexistentialism**. Mexistentialism is short for Mexican existentialism. Like traditional existentialism, it takes seriously the concreteness or facticity of human existence, its situatedness, its finiteness, and its various limitations. Unlike traditional, or European, existentialism, Mexistentialism locates the human struggle in a determinate space-time, one which affects our being human in a definite way, always depending on *where* and *when* one happens to find oneself. For Mexistentialism, that determinate space-time is Mexico, particularly, postcolonial and post-revolutionary Mexico.

The book ends with a section on Questions for Discussion and a list of Further Reading.

Relajo

(rrhe-lah-ho)

Overview of the Concept: *Relajo refers to behaviors or attitudes that bring about the suspension, inversion, or annihilation of the values or meanings, purposefulness or rules, that order or structure events, states of affairs, activities, or many other types of temporally delimited social endeavors. In an abbreviated sense, relajo refers to the suspension of seriousness, when seriousness is understood as that which "holds things together" in certain social contexts. Relajo can thus contribute to the disintegration or breakdown of an otherwise well-ordered or peaceful event or activity by promoting interruptions, the displacements of the audience's attention, or sentiments of chaos and "desmadre" that turn one event into something it was not meant to be. In this way, relajo is destructive.*

On January 6, 2021, supporters of then US president Donald Trump stormed the Capitol building in Washington DC in an effort to overturn the presidential election that Donald Trump had officially lost. What began as a protest meant to pressure legislators into overturning the results quickly escalated into an all-out assault on the US Capitol, where the US Congress was certifying the vote. Flag-waving zealots broke through doors, windows, and all manner of fortifications to get into the congressional chambers; a person was killed in the process (others died afterward). In the end, what had been an insurrection did not achieve its purpose—the final election results stood, as did certain democratic ideals long held as sacrosanct to American culture.

There are differing opinions as to whether or not what transpired on that day was a political insurrection that was carefully planned in advance or, less nefariously, a riot that erupted without warning, one that suddenly broke out like wildfire among individuals who, at the end of the day, were merely caught up in a disruptive and destructive frenzy. Without *obvious* evidence of premeditation (history itself will, perhaps, reveal it), the question into whether or not the chaos of "January 6th" was intentional and carefully planned is not easy to answer. Attorneys for those accused of malicious intent could (and have) argue that their clients had "no intention of rioting . . . but were caught up in the mob" or "overwhelmed by the moment" (Tarm and Billeaud 2021) that as bystanders or onlookers their clients were swept up by a destructive frenzy that seemingly *broke out* without warning, suddenly and out of nowhere.

That this argument is convincing depends on one's politics. However, of interest to us is the notion of being "caught up in" or "overwhelmed by" the moment. What does this mean? Social scientists have recently claimed that the sort of "caught up-ness" witnessed on January 6, 2021, can be explained by, what they call, the "motivational systems theory of group involvement" (Winget and Park 2022). The "theory" explains how a lowering of inhibitions and an intensification of motivation made possible by membership in the crowd or mass led the protesters to riot. The theory assumes, moreover, that group members acted with some sort of reward in mind (e.g., an *intention* to increase their status in the group or an intention to reduce a perceived threat), thus relying on the *psychological* state of those who sought to undermine the electoral process (of those who firmly believed that the nation itself was under threat). However, this theory fails to account for the actions of those who participated in the riot but claim to have had "no intention" of rioting and believe they were merely "caught up in" or "overwhelmed by" *the moment.*

This is an extreme case. But to this and similar, yet less controversial, cases Mexican philosophy offers a term that helps us fill in our current explanatory gap: "relajo."

In our example, the concept of relajo allows us to make sense of *how* a protest that, for all intents and purposes, had no intention of becoming a political insurrection devolved into one or how some participants in the protest were swept up in the frenzy that evolved from it. In such cases, relajo serves as an analytically useful concept that allows us to capture the phenomenon of being *caught up in* or *overwhelmed by* the chaos, unable, afterward, to explain one's actions.

In what follows, I first introduce the notion of "relajo," outlining its intricate architecture as laid out by the Mexican philosopher Jorge Portilla. I will highlight this architecture with some relevant examples. Next, we clear up a misunderstanding that may arise, namely, that relajo may actually be a useful decolonizing strategy. We attempt to clear up the misunderstanding, while not denying relajo's decolonial utility, and return to relajo as a valuable concept for understanding certain aspects of our human experience.

1. Architecture of Relajo

The term "relajo" simply means, *to let go*. As such, the term can be loosely translated into English as "to relax," or the state of being relaxed, since in this state one lets go of stress or pressure—for example, one relaxes on holiday or one relaxes one's grip while holding on to something.[1] As a "letting go," relajo can thus refer to an ungrasping or a "giving up." On this definition, in an attitude of relajo, one's actions can be described (by third parties) as a "giving up" of one's commitment to something, as a being "uncommitted" or, even, "unwilling." Colloquially, as in the Spanish phrase *"echando relajo,"* the term refers to being in a state of *un-commitment*, to a "partying mood" where, if only for a moment, all responsibilities are abandoned and all attachments are *neglected*, and in this neglectful state of partying and dereliction, one suspends one's attachment to the meaning and value of the world. Of course, as "neglect," "abandon," and "dereliction," relajo as a "letting go," *if only momentarily*, is a radical negation, or, as Portilla says, a "suspension of seriousness."

Looked at philosophically, relajo turns out to be a more complex moment of negation, one that Portilla thematizes and subjects to a rigorous phenomenological analysis in his monumental, *La fenomenología del relajo* (translated as *The Phenomenology of Relajo*).[2] Let's now consider what, for Portilla, are its most salient characteristics.

(1.1) *Relajo is the negation of value.*

Portilla subscribes to a functional theory of value.[3] Portilla understands functionalism about values as meaning that values exist insofar as they are "in function with," or together with, things, events, states of affairs, and so on. This means that things, events, or states of affairs will be perceived not as they are in themselves but *through* or *as* their value, which will also be their meaning or significance in a particular context (in phenomenological terms, they will be seen as through a "noematic nucleus" [Portilla 2012, 132, fn. 8]). The value, then, *is useful* as an interface with the world, or as a filter or an interpretive lens through which the perceived makes sense *to us*. Ultimately, values hold the world together, supplying "the meaning that holds [things together] from the inside" (128).

It is values, then, that we suspend, ignore, or neglect in relajo. This is because as the interface with *our* world, values solicit or demand our attention, commitment, and seriousness. In relajo, we say "no" to that demand:

> All value, when grasped, appears surrounded by an aura of demands, endowed with a certain weight and with certain gravity that brings it from its pure ideality toward the world of reality. The value solicits its realization. (129)

In this way, values set limits on our behavior. How we are to behave in a certain situation is always already inscribed in the value through which that situation is seen and understood. If we fail to behave in the way inscribed, or prescribed, by the value of the situation, then we are not acting appropriately in that situation, since we are denying the demands of the value which is in "function with it"; moreover, in this we are also denying the value itself.

Importantly, the value calling for our attention and demanding our action is dependent on our receptivity, on our ability to see it or act in accordance with its demands. Portilla (2012) tells us:

> The mere grasping of the value carries with it the fulfillment of that demand . . . [and its] realization in the world; and in order for this demand . . . to be realized, the subject, in turn, performs an act, a movement of loyalty [to the value] that is a kind of "yes," like an affirmative response. (129)

I respond to the call of values as I encounter them in my daily dealings with objects and states of affairs—even with persons who are seen through values that they themselves represent. By attending to the world in accordance with the perceived values that hold it together, I affirm those values, showing my commitment to them, and saying "yes" to their very existence as well as to every other value associated with them. I reveal, Portilla says, a "duty" to the world in this way, where I "tacitly commit myself to a behavior [and] mortgage my future behavior, making it agree beforehand with that demand: I take the value seriously" (129).

When relajo overwhelms a situation (accounting for being *caught up* in it), it is manifested as the suspension of the values functioning to regulate socially constructed situations. As a suspension of those values, relajo is also the *negation* of values, it is a performative "no" directed to values, social meanings, and expectations that are imposed by culture, society, or history and to which obedience is demanded. Because values are not inherent in the objects or states of affairs, but are only in a certain functional relationship with them, this means that a value has a certain degree of independence. Its independence, however, makes the value vulnerable to manipulation, dislocation, neglect, or defiance. That is, in accordance with the functional theory of value, the value a thing or state of affairs possesses can be dislocated, it can be stripped from it, or it can be "put out of play." Relajo is the actualization of this dislocation, detachment, or deferral.

(1.2) *Relajo is the suspension of seriousness.*

Plainly, to take something seriously is to value that thing; and valuing that thing means that one attends to it in a way that shows reverence or respect to some preconceived story about it. This "story" highlights its value, the reason *why* one attends to it in the way that one does, or again, the reason why one values it. The way Portilla explains this is to say that to take something seriously is to "obey" its demands, which also means one respects the value or values that hold it together.

Returning to our opening example, the institutional story is that living in a democracy involves valuing or taking seriously our electoral system. One does what it demands by voting and respects what it decides, namely, the election results. When one does not vote, engages in fraudulent behavior while voting, or refuses to accept its decisions, one is *disrespecting* that which lends it meaning, its value—when one does such things one is said to "not take it seriously." Portilla puts it like this:

> The sense of relajo is precisely to frustrate the effectiveness of [a] spontaneous response that accompanies the grasping of the value. Relajo suspends seriousness; that is to say, it cancels the normal response to the value, freeing me from the commitment to its realization. (129–30)

So we can ask how one "normally" responds to value. The normal response is the one that most people have or the response that is expected from those taking the value seriously. For instance, the normal response to a lecture is attentive listening while the professor speaks, nodding when one agrees, raising one's hand when there's a question. The abnormal response, on the other hand, is talking loudly to one's classmate about a topic unrelated to the lecture, laughing loudly, or getting up and walking around while talking to oneself. While these abnormal responses are not yet relajo, as we will see later, relajo similarly "cancels" our normal response to what is otherwise a serious situation.

(1.3) *Relajo is a displacement of attention.*

According to William James (1890), attention is "taking possession of . . . an object or train of thought" (403–4). This "taking possession" of something that may be either internal or external to consciousness means that one becomes attached to it in a direct, and immediate, way. In Portilla's philosophy, this "something" is *value* and attention is taking possession of it.

As conscious beings, we attend to our world. This means that in our daily routines we must interact with different aspects of it, and if we are serious about those routines, "taking possession" of those values so as to do those things "right." In relajo, however, we "let go" of our possessions, that is, of values, losing them in a distraction or the chaos of the moment. We will say, in such cases, that we "lost focus." What has happened in this loss of focus is that our attention has been displaced. According to Portilla, this displacement of attention is also a digression and a deviation from our normal response to values. Thus, relajo, besides a suspension of seriousness, is also a displacement, digression, and deviation of attention.

Let's turn to a somewhat extreme ordinary example. Imagine a gathering where attendees seek to address issues relevant to the welfare and security of their community. The gathering itself is a communal space reserved for the rational deliberation of previously agreed upon democratic principles and processes that allow for individual and communal flourishing; it is a space organized by procedural rules and shared practices of respect and generosity. We can say that this gathering space is a space constituted by *values*; it is, moreover a *valuable* space demanding seriousness and respect. To enter into the communal space is to implicitly agree to respect and honor its values and assume responsibility for their fulfillment—that is, to walk into the gathering space is to agree to obey its rules and make sure its values are respected by oneself and by others.

Now imagine that as the gathering gets underway, and while members are fully engaged in an open and rational discussion about, for instance, the equitable distribution of water, someone whispers jokingly that "some people obviously need less of it," suggesting with that comment that bathing is not everyone's priority. Someone hears it and laughs; someone scoffs; somebody voices agreement; someone wonders what was said; the comment is repeated. What had been a serious discussion comes to a sudden stop. Everyone turns toward the source of the whisper. Talk of resource distribution is replaced with disorganized chatter about who takes baths, who looks like they need one, and so on; some members wonder if the comment was meant for them. There is giggling, laughing, shouting, and talking over one another. The rules and procedures that previously held together the otherwise rational deliberation about resource allocation seem to have evaporated; there is mayhem and disorder. Seriousness is suspended. Attachment to, or solidarity with, the value of the gathering is dislocated. We have here a deviation, digression, or displacement of attention away from what the communal gathering was about. A simple comment brought about a complete loss of focus, the negation of values, and the suspension of seriousness. We say that *the gathering devolved into relajo.*

Looking at what happened, we see that the original displacement of attention, the first utterance, was *not yet* relajo. Relajo, as we will see (1.6, later) is a communal act. The first utterance, however, was not a "normal response" to what was being "seriously" discussed, so this first utterance was a first, and significant, movement toward it. Relajo fully set in only when others joined in the displacement of attention by focusing on the comment and away from what the meeting was "about"—away from its value. For this reason Portilla refers to the displacement of attention as the "axis around which the entire *moral* meaning of relajo revolves" (130), since any direct or indirect harm caused by the dissolution of the value holding the gathering together can be traced to the initial displacement or the initial interruption, that is, to the moment that initiated the chaos.

So far, relajo can be broken up into three moments: (1.1) the negation of value, (1.2) the suspension of seriousness, and, now,

(1.3) the displacement of attention. While there are other moments characterizing relajo (for instance, that it involves an invitation to others to participate in its negations, (1.6)), at the heart of the phenomenon, is (1.3), the displacement of attention, characterized as a "digression" or "deviation" from the value to which one ought to be attending, to something other or external to our serious concerns.

(1.4) *Relajo's Bi-Intentionality*

The idea that one could find oneself "caught up" in relajo just like one could get "caught up in a storm" or "caught up in traffic," suggests that relajo is a sort of "mindless," "purposeless" fog into which one can easily fall. But relajo is not mindless or purposeless like fog is mindless or purposeless. Relajo is, in fact, purposeful and intentional.

The sort of intentionality that characterizes relajo, however, is not the intellectual, mental or cognitive *consciousness of*, or a simple directedness toward an object, that Husserl describes (Husserl 2001). It involves, rather, what Portilla calls "double intentionality." Double intentionality is an intentionality directed at two places at once: at the displacement or the negation of those values holding together a serious situation and, simultaneously, at possible accomplices to the displacement or negation. It is an intentionality that shoots forward and sideways at the same time. Portilla (2012) puts it this way:

> Concurrent with the negative intentionality toward the value, there emerges a "lateral" intentionality toward others, which is as necessary as the former to constitute the essence of the phenomenon of relajo. (132)

Evidence for the double intentionality of relajo is found in the example of the communal gathering interrupted by the comment about those needing baths. First we find the act that initiates the displacement of attention away from deliberation about communal resources is *consciously directed* at that value in a negative way—it *seeks* to move us away from that value and suspend the seriousness of the discussion. Second yet simultaneously, pre-reflectively and *performatively*, the comment seeks (even if the speaker *did not* seek) to involve others in the dislocation; the gestures, tone, and physicality of the utterance that gives rise to relajo *aims* to transform listeners into accomplices in the repetition of the act. Portilla calls the first, "negative intentionality toward the value" and, the second, "lateral" intentionality "toward others," both, he continues, are "necessary" for the constitution "of the essence of the phenomenon of relajo."[4]

(1.5) *Relajo maintains itself through repetition.*

The dislocation of attention essential to relajo requires an initial act of disruption that engages the bi-intentionality of the act, that double intentionality that lures others into the suspensions of seriousness and negation of values. But this "lateral" intentionality is effective only if there is a repetition of that initial act, a recurrence that creates a *scene*; this repetition is, Portilla says, "a negative backdrop that makes [the fulfillment of value] impossible or useless" (134).

Essential to relajo is that it is "reiterated action" (133). Portilla describes this phenomenon as follows:

> A single joke that, for example, interrupts the speech delivered by a speaker is not enough to transform the interruption into relajo. The suspensive interruption of seriousness must be repeated indefinitely whether or not the agent of relajo archives his or her purpose. It is necessary for the interrupting gesture or word to be repeated continuously until the dizzying thrill of complicity in negation takes over the group, which is the most paradoxical of all communities: a community of non-communicators. (133–4)

In our example, relajo fully sets in when the discussion about water allocation devolves into a comic episode about who takes baths and how often. The devolution itself is driven by the repetition of the initial comment and the continual suspension or negation of what was originally the central theme of the discussion—the distribution or allocation of resources. It was not enough for one person to utter something off-topic; someone else had to repeat it, and then someone else, and so on, in order for the creation of a scene in which rational deliberation became "impossible or useless."

Portilla says that one joke, for instance, is not enough for a scene to devolve into relajo. The joke must be repeated "indefinitely," whether or not anyone laughs. In our gathering, the "dizzying thrill of complicity in negation" is achieved when those that would otherwise be participating in a rational discussion about communal resources find themselves fervently defending themselves or their hygiene. The scene is thrilling, dizzying, and one can easily get caught up, or swept up in it. In the example of the riotous mob with which we started, it is likely that some participants were "swept" up in the mayhem and in the negating "complicity" without realizing that they were, in fact, unwitting insurrectionists.

(1.6) *Relajo is a social act.*

To be "caught up" or "swept up" in an insurrection or in the disruption of a rational discussion about communal resources implies a communal setting. Relajo can only happen in the space of community or with others. Portilla tells us that an individual, on his own, cannot bring about relajo: "[r]elajo in solitude is unthinkable, or, I should say, unimaginable" (132). This is because, according to Portilla, the "dimension of depth, that quasi-space in which relajo can proliferate like parasitic vegetation" is missing (133). Like a parasite, relajo requires a host; relajo's host is *any* circumstance where two or more are gathered.

Relajo's double intentionality, together with its requirement for repetition, points to its social dimension. Portilla observes that "the characteristic of 'action,' essential to relajo, points back in turn to another essential element: relajo can only present itself in a horizon of community" (132). Moreover, given its bi-intentionality, "[i]f relajo is an attitude toward a value, it is also . . . an attitude that indirectly alludes to 'others'" (132). This means that "[t]he invocation to others is . . . an essential constituent of relajo" (133).

Ultimately, that new and unexpected scene, or that "an atmosphere in which the realization of value is definitely thwarted" (134), can only be created through repetition and the thrill of complicity in negation which can only happen in the presence of others, which are, in turn, its hosts and actors.

(1.7) *Relajo is liberating but not revolutionary.*

As a *suspension of seriousness*, a *displacement of attention*, and an *inversion of values*, relajo can be a destructive act. It can destroy an otherwise stable relation between a subject and her commitment to those values that organize and hold her world together. Along with undermining this relation, relajo also appears to *destroy* value itself— we have used words like negation, annihilation, suspension, and so on, words that suggest this destruction. In this way, the aftermath of relajo is imagined as a barren landscape lacking values and order. Portilla writes:

> [Relajo] renders effective action difficult or impossible, but also, with its negativity, it erases the motivation of the action itself: the value. *Relajo* kills action in its cradle. It negates the only thing that gives sense to action; it prevents the light of value from illuminating the scaffolding of . . . means and ends that would lead to the action's realization. *Relajo* is a paradoxically inactive that renders the value's call sterile. (188–9)

It's not farfetched to assume, from this and what has been previously said, that relajo is the perfect response to the coloniality of power embodied in the historicity of values or imposed ways of life. If relajo is the behavior of individuals in the colonial world, then this behavior, in suspending seriousness, in negating values, and in dislocating attention, is decolonizing if for the simple fact that it destroys our adherence to values inherited from colonialism. In this sense, relajo is a destructive yet liberating phenomenon. Portilla, however, discourages us from thinking of it in this way.

> After relajo, things remain exactly the same as before. Because of this, relajo cannot be considered a "revolutionary" attitude . . . Its indisputable effectiveness consist in making another's action ineffective. (189)

While it may be temporarily destructive, and liberating, relajo is not revolutionary. After all, it is merely a "suspension" of values. As merely suspended, what is negated is only put out of play. On this reading, relajo could never initiate a revolutionary act of decolonization, since, in *suspending* seriousness, it does not annihilate its object; in general, relajo leaves colonial structures intact.

(1.8) *To relajo correspond relajientos (and snobs)*

There are persons that exist to bring about relajo. They are called "relajientos."

Relajientos, in personifying relajo, are thought to be the enemies of seriousness. They are known in the community as those that do not take anything seriously, not even themselves, but especially social rules or conventions. If they come across a serious situation, like a gathering where a result or achievement of some kind is expected—they will not go in search of it, since this would mean that they take *something* seriously—they will waste no time interrupting it in some way that will deny its value, suspend its seriousness, or negate its purpose.

Because they take nothing seriously, not even themselves, the relajiento is not hard to spot; there is, Portilla says, a "certain way about them." We would say that the relajiento is extremely chill, relaxed, uncommitted, and even lazy. Meeting them, one notices that they are unbothered by worries or commitments, and their speech and behavior suggest that what they value most of all is the freedom to do as they please. They are, in this way, an extreme sort of existentialist: they live fully in the now because there is no future purpose that orients their lives. Portilla tells us that "relajiento is, literally, an individual without a future. . . . he or she refuses to take anything seriously, to commit to anything . . . assumes no responsibility for anything . . . a good humor witness to the banality of life" (147).

We know relajientos when we see them, and we see them coming from a mile away. As they approach, the atmosphere fills with tension, as their arrival threatens to distract us, or to get us "off track." Portilla describes it like this:

> Their mere presence is a foreshadowing of the dissolution of any possible seriousness. Their mere appearance unleashes a light breeze of smiles and the atmosphere is transformed into a condescending expectation of a shower of jokes that will dissolve the seriousness of all topics, reducing them literally, to nothing . . . This individual is a 'relajiento.'" (147)

With words, jokes, taunts, looks, movements of the face, arms, or legs, a loud yell, and so on, the relajiento can bring to a halt an entire scene. As the scene threatens to unravel, two things may happen: one, the relajiento is intercepted, kicked out, putting a stop to the devolution before it starts; or, two, someone else repeats the action, the yell, the joke, and so on, and then a third person, until the scene devolves into something it was not meant to be, "an endless rosary of negated moments" (147). In such negated moments, our attention seems to be under attack, and negations colonize our space; the values that hold the space together are suspended and reduced to "nothing," or, in other words, they can no longer do what values are supposed to do. What the scene pretended to be before the appearance of the relajiento is now not the same scene. It is an *other* scene, a valueless and chaotic scene.

One thinks back to childhood friends or acquaintances that were surely relajientos. We all had them. They were fun companions, since when in their company, nothing was taken seriously, everything was joking, play, and the abandonment of worries. They certainly took us out of time and concern. As Portilla puts it: "[t]he relajiento does not bring about preoccupation but rather inoccupation" (147–8). However, this inoccupation or playfulness depends or relies on a negation, that is, on the destruction of values and the suspension of a seriousness, those things that not only structure the now but also serve as guides into the future *as expectation*. This, perhaps, explains why those childhood friends are no longer our friends. We somehow knew that they, and the relajo they brought about, were obstacles to our own futures.

It is worth emphasizing that while the relajiento embodies the qualities of relajo, he is not *relajo itself*. Although he may *threaten* relajo's arrival, on his own, he simply brings with him this "threat." In his mannerisms, and in his language, he simply refuses commitments or seriousness. In doing so, he also refuses the demands of history, time, and community. But he is not relajo, since more is needed for relajo to take root (see earlier). Nonetheless, as an individual, he can't be oppressed or repressed, since he refuses and negates the language and the mechanisms of power inherent in inherited values. In the end, however, the relajiento is not so much an enemy of social norms, customs, and values, but, because relajo is his mode of being, he is his own worst enemy. As Portilla says, the relajiento's "systematic negation of value is [ultimately] a movement of self-destruction" (149).

Now we get to the "apretado," which we find in, Portilla says, "the absolute opposite pole" in relation to the relajiento. The apretado, which we can translate as "snob" or "zealot," is serious, or, better yet, *burdened with seriousness* to the point that he is "tightly wound," always occupied, and fully committed to his beliefs. According to Portilla, these individuals are "afflicted with the spirit of seriousness" (190), which means that they will take themselves and what they find important (i.e., what they value) extremely, or excessively, serious. Such commitment to seriousness will set them apart.

Unlike the relajiento whose only value is the negative freedom to do as he pleases, the apretado prefers order, seriousness, and commitment—but, again, to an excessive degree.

> Deep down, apretados love order more than freedom. Order is that stable situation of society that allows these individuals to play the exclusivity game and to give themselves the pleasure of embodying value. The objective expression of that order is Law. (196)

As such, the apretado lives to participate in the law, which makes possible the order necessary for the fulfillment of values, some of which he embodies in the way he dresses, speaks, and acts. We could say that he is "fanatical" about those values. In him, one finds "no distance . . . between being and value"—the apreatado *is* what he values, and he wears it on his face, his clothes, his bumper stickers, and his hats because these are "an expression of his internal being" (191). Apretados "carry their value in the same way that they carry with them their legs or their liver: as a silent and solid cause of pleasure that they caress in their private moments." (191) They are, Portilla says, "[c]ompact masses of value." (191).

Notice that both of these personality types are defined by their relation to value. This relation, in both cases, is excessive and extreme: the relajiento relates to value in a negative, destructive, way while the apretado's relation is one of obsession and embodiment. Portilla argues that such extremism and excessiveness are, ultimately, destructive of the community. He writes:

> Both the freedom of the "apretado" individual and that of the "relajiento" are negative freedoms. That is why, in both attitudes there is a negation of community. One and the other dissolve the community—which can only be founded upon a value that is transcendental to its members. (198)

Believing themselves to be absolutely free to do as they please without interference (i.e., believing their freedom to be a negative freedom), both relajientos and apretados act against the best interests of the community to which they belong, the first by disobeying the dictates of the community's grounding, "transcendental," values and the second by being absolutists about how they understand these values, rigidly and close-mindedly reading them in their own way while demanding fanatical obedience to this reading.

For the sake of illustration, consider two different hypothetical communities:

The first, a community which has fallen to neglect. Here, violence and crime are rampant, roads are unkempt, and homes are in various states of disrepair. While a "transcendental vision" of prosperity and flourishing for the community exists, it goes unfulfilled in spite of the best efforts of organizers, City Hall, and its residents. Outside observers notice that every effort to implement this "vision" is challenged by interruptions and disturbances that force projects, investments, and improvements to stop or change focus. Observers pick out a few individuals responsible for the interruptions and disturbances. These are the relajientos for whom the "transcendental vision" of the community others strive to fulfill is of no consequence, of no value. They are easy to pick out because, according to Portilla, relajientos "detest order and destroy it every time [they] can" (147). In this way, relajientos, bring about disorder and destruction and are responsible for the dissolution of the community's transcendental vision.

The second is a gated community with manicured lawns and a somewhat tyrannical Home Owners Association (HOA). Those that live here appreciate the location, the nearby schools, the low crime rate, and the feeling of safety. For them, this is an ideal place to live, where family, freedom, *and* security are tantamount values. But it comes at a cost. Everyone must conform to the HOA rules or be fined, perhaps even expelled. The HOA president has his own vision for the community, and no deviations are allowed. He values freedom and security but believes one must come at the expense of the other. Residents recognize their loss of freedom but say and do nothing, as they would rather live under this tyranny than anywhere else. The "transcendental values" of the community, those that, in their heart, residents appreciate are eclipsed by a singular vision of perfection and obedience, represented by the HOA president whose entire identity is that of being "HOA president."

This hypothetical example, although a bit abstract, points to extreme poles in a possible relation to value. Portilla concludes his *Phenomenology of Relajo* by reminding us that neither of the character types described can serve as ideal members of a properly functioning, or genuine, community. The last sentence reads: "'Relajinetos and apretados' constitute two poles of dissolution of that difficult task on which we have all embarked: the constitution of a . . . a genuine community" (199).

Much can be said about the middle ground between these two extremes. For now, this should suffice: between the nihilism of the relajiento and the fanaticism of the apretado there is a politically, morally, and existentially preferable way to be. This middle ground will be the personality type that respects societal values, obeys communal rules, laws, and prohibitions, but is willing to question and challenge her situation, changing her mind if necessary. This middle-ground personality will use irony and humor to her advantage as a means to reveal the right way to be and the right way to go, and not as a weapon of disruption or suspension (she will not be a relajiento). Moreover, she will identify with values, but will not become them, and will always be willing to be rationally led to other, more enriching, values and ways of being (she will not be an apretado).

2. On Liberation, Revolution, and Decolonization: Application of the Concept

Despite Portilla's suggestion that relajo is negative and harmful to community in general and to the integrity of values in particular, one could reimagine the concept as liberatory, perhaps, even, embodying a practice of decolonization. Although we've already discussed how Portilla does not think this to be the case, it is nonetheless worthwhile to consider this possibility.

A principal strategy of colonization is domination through the destruction and supplanting of native values. Through violent processes of displacement and replacement new obediential structures are grafted onto existing social relations. Colonialism succeeds when those structures—in the form of values meant to control and determine behavior and social order—are codified into the everyday world and become the filter through which that world is understood and lived. The end result of this process is that the colonized themselves come to consider the supplanted values as inferior to the supplanting, foreign, values. To take them seriously is to perpetuate the belief in their superiority and, in effect, perpetuate coloniality. To reject them is to challenge that superiority and, in effect, challenge coloniality.

In simple terms, colonialism involves and requires the imposition of values and the regulation of seriousness maintained in colonial relations, institutions, and structures that are then passed down from one generation to the next. In such a context, relajo threatens the maintenance and continuity of an established and inherited colonial axiology. Inherited values are displaced in suspensions and the "thrill of complicity in negation" essential to the *moment, event,* or *scene* of relajo. This suspension, dislocation, or negation puts the values out of play, and with that, that force and power that defines a continued colonial system, what Anibal Quijano (2000) calls, the "coloniality of power." In such conditions, relajo appears as an anti-colonial or de-colonial maneuver that, even if spontaneous, unexpected, and momentary, nonetheless denies, for instance, a 500-year-old imposition and the ever-present power of coloniality. In this sense, relajo seems liberatory; it liberates the colonialized subject from the shackles of those colonial demands that, once imposed, survive to the present.

Consider the unproblematic act of walking into a Catholic church for Sunday mass. Let's imagine it is a sixteenth-century baroque cathedral with thick walls and high ceilings, decorated from corner to corner and floor to ceiling with gold-plated frames of saints and scenes from Christ's Passion; the place is dark and smells of incense and burned candles. The worshipers take their seats. Almost 2,000 years of rules and rituals thicken the air and crowd into the 500 years old building. There are thus values here that *must* be obeyed, respected, and brought to fulfillment through the actions of the supplicants. One must pray, quietly and reverently, while focused on nothing else but the unimaginable suffering of Christ on the Cross. What one must do and say has been scripted in advance—centuries in advance, and one must not go off script, something that would be an act of disrespect and contempt against the Church, Christ, oneself, and one's community. One feels the value that holds the entire scene together as one feels the damp air, it is in the atmosphere, dominating the space. It seems solid, and weighty, like a physical thing. Now imagine an individual for whom these rituals, that is, values, seem frivolous and oppressive. Rather than bow his head in obedience to tradition, that is, to values, he loudly proclaims that *Mexico's World Cup chances are, actually, not that bad this year and maybe we should pray for victory.* While this outburst displaces the attention of the worshipers, it is not yet relajo. Someone in the back, however, follows up that *Mexico's World Cup team won't make it past the second round.* Another adds that *maybe neither of you have seen the new squad.* Immediately, a discussion breaks out about Mexican soccer and attention has been diverted away from Christ on the Cross and to Mexico in the World Cup. Some people laugh, others shush, and others silently wonder *if, in fact, Mexico has a chance against Germany this year.* Relajo has set in. Through its bi-intentionality, the diversion spreads through the entire congregation; the Priest gives up and retreats. The values inherent in Catholic worship are suspended. If only for a moment, the colonial values that have dominated the discourse and behavior in *this particular place* for almost 500 years have been overcome via a series of negations and displacements. Here, relajo appears as a decolonial weapon.

Certainly, on this account, the promise of a sustained suspension of values could attract community (via relajo's bi-intentionality or double intentionality) and thus open up channels of communication through which the liberatory act could, possibly, become a revolutionary event. Relajo *could* become the way to overthrow a certain colonial system once and for all (if, that is, its suspension were carried out with every single colonial value making up that system). However, this kind of sustained and focused suspension of values is not possible in relajo for at least three reasons:

1. the temporality of relajo is truncated;
2. multiple relajo events may instantiate simultaneously; and,
3. negated values are not replaced in the process of displacement.

Let's consider each of these in turn.

1. *Relajo's temporal horizon is truncated.* In Portilla's account, relajo "requires an occasion, which is to say, the appearance of a value that offers itself to the subject's freedom and from which a dissent can begin" (130). In other words, the *event* of a value's appearance (e.g., one which inherited, established, a colonial value) is the scene or setting for relajo to unravel. This scene or setting, however, is temporally bounded, determined by time *and* space, and will play out in accordance to a finite temporal horizon, just as the event of the value's appearance "to the subject's freedom." This is why relajo requires repetition, or constant repetitive initiations, so that it may persist *long enough* to keep the value in suspension. However, this also means that a scene or event of relajo will last so long as the repetitions and interruptions of value and seriousness persist; once these lose momentum and the repetitions cease, so does relajo. Of relajo's three moments (see 1.3, earlier), which include the displacement of attention, the lack of solidarity with the value, and the invitation to others to participate in the disruption, none of them suggest a *permanent* digression from what originally demanded one's attention or obedience. The suspension of value is simply that, a *suspension*, and what is suspended will return once again, on another occasion, for another event. Hence, an inherited colonial value (say, Catholic reverence) may be suspended or displaced in relajo, but this suspension or displacement will last as long as relajo, after which the value will reset, and its rules and demands will continue demanding seriousness, respect, or observance.

2. *Multiple relajo events may instantiate simultaneously, interrupting and displacing each other in the process.* To say, as we do, that it is possible to sustain the occasion of relajo through cycles of repetition, is to assign a purposeful intentionality to the event of relajo itself; namely, that it is aiming to accomplish *something*, usually the displacement of attention. However, as an event now endowed with its own value (and with its own intentionality), it is possible that it too be interrupted by another relajo event simultaneous to itself. For this reason, a relajo event cannot properly establish itself as its own unique event. Its distractions and displacements are spontaneous and, because the displaced value

is *not* immediately replaced, its absence, or the negative space this absence creates, makes further digressions possible. In creating and then becoming this negative space, relajo itself becomes vulnerable to repeated invasions, evasions, and interference. In our example, the disruption of colonial values cannot turn into a decolonial practice since "practice" implies an order and organization made impossible by relajo's very essence. In simple terms, a permanent relajo event is unsustainable because *it cannot be kept up*.

3. *In relajo, what is displaced is not replaced.* Portilla tells us that "[a]fter relajo, things remain exactly the same as before" (188). The suspension of seriousness that suspends the efficacy of a value accomplishes neither its complete destruction nor its replacement. When, in the "thrill of complicity" one refuses the call of a value and displaces one's attention away from it, the value is taken out of play; but this "taking out of play" only means that the value is no longer effective in the moment or occasion. The value will return to its place when the displacement ends. In the meantime, nothing takes its place. There is *nothing* in its place. Portilla writes that the displacement of value "is only a change in the intentional object of consciousness and not a deliberate act in which the subject will 'concentrate on a new object.'" (130). This speaks also to the previous point. The idea here is that a new object of attention will not replace what is merely suspended; what is suspended is not obliterated, it is only *taken out of play*.

Consequently, while relajo can be seen as a moment in a more robust decolonial practice, it cannot serve as a model for prolonged decolonization strategies. Relajo is liberating, but only on occasion, in spurts, or momentarily; it is useless as an *effort*. As Portilla says, "[r]elajo kills action in its crib" (188), which means that it cannot be "revolutionary," and ultimately, decolonializing. It may help a protest by contributing to the spectacle necessary to distract attention, but it cannot sustain a movement. Portilla thus thinks that relajo is incompatible with communal flourishing; the nihilism of relajo is not desirable. If values are to be challenged, Portilla endorses a sort of Socratic-irony that we've talked about before and that we will not get into here.[5] Ultimately, if our target is the breaking of colonial relations, we must find a different way to do it; perhaps a way which is more in line with the demands of reason, good thinking, and strategic action.

3. Conclusion

This book seeks to interrupt the Western tradition of philosophy, to displace attention away from that tradition and focus it, if only for a moment, on the post-Western, nepantla tradition that Mexican philosophy represents. But this book is not an instance of relajo. It will add something to philosophy—it seeks to be creative and not merely destructive. In this, it seeks to do a bit of decolonization. I find this creative definition of decolonization in Franz Fanon's *The Wretched of the Earth*. There, Fanon (2004) writes:

> Decolonization never goes unnoticed, for it focuses on and fundamentally alters being, and transforms the spectator crushed to a nonessential state into a privileged actor, captured in a virtually grandiose fashion by the spotlight of History. It infuses a new rhythm, specific to a new generation of men, with a new language and a new humanity. Decolonialization is truly the creation of new men. But such a creation cannot be attributed to a supernatural power: The "thing" colonized becomes a man through the very process of liberation. (2)

And so I imagine that this is what I am doing here. By highlighting the value of concepts from Mexican philosophy, I am "infusing a new rhythm" to a "new generation" with a "new language." But this is sustained, multigenerational work, with a purpose and a strategy. Again, this effort is not relajo (although it is vulnerable to it, as all purposeful, value-filled, efforts). Ultimately, given Fanon's definition one cannot think that all manner of rejection of colonial values is properly decolonial. As Fanon clearly points out, decoloniality can only come about with sustained effort, and when completed, it will give us something "new." The phenomenon of relajo is not decolonial in this, Fanonian sense, although it can flare up in the course of such movements.

The last sentence reminds us that relajo is not negative through and through. It is, after all, a release, a letting go, that can unburden one (however briefly) from pressures of having to succumb to the constant demand of values. In relajo we are freed from our commitments, enjoying, for a moment, a liberation into chaos. Moreover, relajo is also diagnostic. In our contemporary world, it reveals the fragile and brittle nature of order and civility. Seeing how easily a relajo event can upend the social contract is sobering and should force us, as a society, to reevaluate our most sacred institutions. Or, we can go inward, as relajo also reveals a societal attention deficit disorder whereby the "thrill of complicity in negation" is too much to pass up. This may indicate that, perhaps, we do not care as much as we should. And this, I think, is a more worrisome matter.

2

Nepantla

(ne-pant-lah)

Overview of the Concept: *Nepantla describes existence as in-between identities, temporalities, or states of being. As a state of being, it is not a ground or foundation which defines one as either this or that, but an undifferentiated space of convergence and divergence, of suspension, pendularity, and unsettledness inside of which our identity—our "I" or "we"—struggles, overcomes, grows and decays; in this way, nepantla defines one as undefined. Simply put, one exists as nepantla when one refuses (on purpose or accidentally) to "fit" perfectly in the world, to do what the world's "perfection" demands, or to settle into "the world" when this appears always as unfamiliar, unwelcoming, or threatening. Members of marginalized communities of all kinds often exist as nepantla.*

The concept of "nepantla" has an established historiography in English-language Latinx scholarship. Primarily associated with Latinx/Chicanx feminism, and in particular with the work of Gloria Anzaldúa, it has come to name the social, political, and gendered status of those who live "in-between" traditionally articulated worlds, in-between gendered and linguistic spaces, in-between differential sites of oppression and marginalization, and so on.

However, the concept has a longer history outside of this historiography, one intertwined with the Nahuatl experience of European colonization and displacement. Without getting too deep into that history, our aim here is to lend this concept coherence and project its future, one which is not necessarily political nor cultural but applicable to many other subjectivities or subjective experiences.

My claim is that the future of this concept is a *philosophical* future describing human experience in its concreteness and contingency.

1. What Is "Nepantla"?

Understanding *nepantla* means accepting its polysemy. We can understand it by one, a few, or all of the following characterizations:

(i) Nepantla is an ontological concept that refers to a *suspension between commitments or worlds* that is indicative of the "postmodern" tendency toward indetermination, fluidity, and accidentality.

(ii) Nepantla captures the *always being on the way*, that is, the nomadism of those in-between worlds, but also of the world-less, those who have been displaced by social, political, or other forces. In the following, I refer to this as its *never again/never yet* structure.

(iii) Nepantla describes an existential *refusal* to commit, a *neutrality* regarding direct action on the circumstances in which some find themselves, circumstances which oftentimes offer no true living option. I'm thinking here of persons who exist with inherited oppressive existential situations and who, considering them as inadequate, refuse to commit themselves to them.

(iv) Finally, nepantla is the "in between" temporalities, worlds, and processes; it is being "in the middle," as in "on the way," in transit, from one place to another, or "in the middle" as in "in the midst of" a crisis or a paradigm shift.

These different ways to characterize the phenomenon revolve around a central axis, summarized neatly in the phrase "to be nepantla is to be *in-between*." Because there are many kinds of "in-betweenness" across multiple human experiences, nepantla can be deployed outside the established historiography (whether Mexican or Latinx). Our aim, in fact, is to propose nepantla as a category of human experience with a much broader, and global, application.

Some may find my proposal troubling. It is troubling because to offer nepantla to the world seems like an expropriation. That is, it appears as if I am stripping it from the Latinx/Chicanx self-narrative, which, it could be argued, is one expropriation, one theft, too many. So why do it? Simply, out of a sense of duty to a tradition impoverished by its own Anglo-eurocentrism. Enriching it means multiplying its vocabularies and diversifying its sources—some of which have been here all along. Here is a concept, original to the Americas, that fits our modern and postmodern condition like a glove, but which, perhaps out of ignorance or racist assumptions has been marginalized by the history of thought (see Introduction). So, even if it is not *my* gift to give, I believe nepantla captures something essential about our contemporariness, one that makes it useful for whomever shares in that all-too-human experience.

2. "... *todavía estamos nepantla*."

The term "nepantla" is first recorded by Andrés de Olmos (1485–1571) in *Arte de la lengua mexicana*, a dictionary of the Indigenous-Spanish language from 1547. It later reappears in a more popular dictionary by the Franciscan Friar Alonso de Molina (1513–79) in 1571 (Troncoso 2011, 377). Molina gives us a sense of the centrality of the term in the náhuatl language. We find it in words signifying "the center of the earth," *tlalli nepantla*, "messenger," *nepantla quiza titlantli*, "divide into two," *nepantla tequi, nitla*, "noon," *nepantla tonatiuh*, and "between extremes," *nepantlatli*, to name a few (Thouvenot 2014, 213). The practical significance of the term, however, is suggested by Dominican Friar Diego Durán's (1537–88) "New World" chronicle of 1581, *History of the Indies of New Spain* (Durán 1994). Durán's account allows us to encounter the term in context. Approximately 400 years later, Emilio Uranga uses Durán's account as an epigraph to his *Analysis of Mexican Being*:

> As I listened to an Indian tell me of certain things, and in particular that he had dragged himself on the ground picking up money on bad

nights and worse days, and once he had, with much effort, collected a certain amount of money he had a wedding and invited the entire town, and as I rebuked him for the Evil he had done, he answered: "Father, don't be alarmed, since we are still nepantla [*porque todavía estamos nepantla*]." And while I understood what he meant to say with that vocabulary and that metaphor, which means to be in the middle, I turned and insisted that he tell me what middle it was in which they were, he told me that since they were not very well rooted in faith, that I shouldn't be alarmed since they were still neutral in the sense that they neither depended on one law or another, or better put, that they believed in God and at the same time relied on their ancient customs and demonic rites [*costumbres antiguas y ritos del demonio*], and this is what he meant with that abominable excuse that they still remained in the middle and were neutral. (Uranga 2021, 92; Durán 1994, 237)

Durán translation, while filtered through his own ideological lens (what we will call a "figure of the world" in Chapter 6), retains nepantla's basic meaning, namely, as a being "in the middle" of two moral universes ("laws") but beholden to neither and, in a certain sense, *free* from them. His ideological lens is clearer, however, as he considers that the indigenous man is giving an "abominable excuse" actually rooted in a state of being where he feels himself ontologically (and *ethically*) suspended over two distinct ontological domains. This allows us to read further into the encounter, and interpret nepantla as a being untethered to a ground, a floating or hoovering over boundaries of distinct domains without being anchored on any of them. Thus, nepantla points to an existence in motion, one which is uncommitted, unsettled, and undefined.

As one who finds oneself "unanchored" to a ground, moreover, to be nepantla is to be morally, politically, and spiritually "neutral." To be neutral is to unbiased and uncommitted to this or that point of view; to be neutral is to be capable of choosing either, neither, or both. It is to experience an uncanny (and, perhaps, frightening) sort of freedom. In Durán's encounter, the indigenous man, in declaring his neutrality, his middlehood, is also declaring himself free from the obligation to either "God," on the one hand, or "the demonic," on the other. His purgatory—his nepantla—is unregulated by the laws of either. In saying that "we are still nepantla," he is articulating the belief that they are *still* (*todavía*) traversing the space from one to another—from the demonic to God—and are *not yet* in either one or the other. Indigenous life, Durán is told abruptly, exists in a persistent state of suspension and transition (from the old to the new or, even, the new to the old), in transit toward an unknown "yet," suspended "in the middle" of a (what will be a catastrophic) paradigm shift.[1] This is a state, moreover, to which the indigenous man has gotten used to; a sentiment reflected in his attempt to comfort the "alarmed" priest: "Father," he says, "don't be alarmed, *todavía estamos nepantla*."[2]

3. Nepantla in Mexican Philosophy

The introduction of nepantla as a philosophical concept represents a moment of rupture between Mexican philosophy and the Western tradition. With this concept, it forgoes imitation in favor of originality. Its introduction, furthermore, represents the intervention, interruption, and imposition of a genuinely American philosophical category on the Western tradition, a category that emerges from the precolonial indigenous experience, yet is applicable to other experiences. Uranga writes: "We thus have before us, in all its purity, the central category of our ontology, autochthonous, one that does not borrow from the Western tradition, satisfying our desire to be originalists" (Uranga 2021, 167). It is in the sense of its being an original contribution that it is appropriated by both Uranga Elsa Cecilia Frost to characterize *modern* Mexican culture and identity. Let's consider its use in both Uranga and Frost.

3.1. Ontological Nepantla

Nepantla is mentioned only twice in the main text of Emilio Uranga's *Analysis of Mexican Being*, yet it is arguably the most significant "ontological" concept in his philosophical arsenal. The concept first appears in the second of the epigraphs that open up his study. It reappears in the final part, Part IV, of *Analysis* where he writes:

> The Mexican character does not install itself over . . . two agencies, but between [*entre*] them. The nahuatl term "*nepantla*" captures this phenomenon perfectly; it means "in between," in the middle, in the center. We thus have before us, in all its purity, the central category of our ontology, autochthonous, one that does not borrow from the Western tradition.(2021, 167)

As "the central category of [a Mexican] ontology," nepantla defies the Western philosophical tradition by insisting on the ontological priority of indeterminateness and non-identity. Proposing it as such is an important strategic move for Uranga, since motivating his analysis of Mexican being is an attempt to confront colonial stubborn prejudices and conceptualizations. For instance, the colonial notion of Mexicans as inferior to Europeans due to cultural and historical mestizaje, itself due to racist notions of purity, is met with a concept that insists that mestizaje, and, thus, impurity, point to that which defines *authentic human life* as always already becoming, as constant movement, change, and contingency.

The image that the Mexica (Aztecs) used to represent nepantla was that of a rabbit, or more accurately, a rabbit on the run (Uranga 2013, 148).[3] A rabbit on the run, for example, one fleeing from a predator, does not run in a straight line but jumps from side to side, zigzagging so as to escape capture. The Mexica identified with the rabbit, imagining their own being as reflecting a certain "rabbithood" [*empeño conejeril*] (149), defined by a constant or persistent state of vigilance or flight, by existing as an evasion, always avoiding the gaze of the other, the conqueror, or the schemes of the imposed culture. The familiar rabbit thus adequately symbolized the indigenous condition after the Spanish conquest and the persecutions that followed—one had to be evasive, elusive, and hard to catch, a being that "jumped from here to there, that never stays in one place" (148). Although they would not escape their fate, the Mexica would not be easy to capture, to pin down, or to domesticate. While these analogies have their limit, Uranga writes that they are nonetheless "invaluable to us, because they show that iridescent or half-tone structure [of] our true being" (148). Following the Mexica, Uranga conceives nepantla, ultimately, as a state of being *un-installed*, un-grounded, and un-finished ("in the middle" referring, in this way, to being between points, to transition).

Thus nepantla describes an original or originary state of being—that is, an authentic mode of being human in a post-Western sense. This sets nepantla apart from zozobra (see Chapter 3). While "zozobra," as we will see, refers to the emotive aspect of this state of being, nepantla simply refers to this being in-transition, in-between, on the way, suspended, and so on.[4]

With Uranga, Mexican philosophy recovers and re-appropriates the Nahuatl concept of "nepantla" as an ontological concept. While the original Nahuatl concept described a being "in-between" a past denied (i.e., the indigenous past) and a present imposed (i.e., European laws and culture), on the other, it now describes modern Mexican existence as a being "in between" a past affirmed (i.e., the reality of 500 years of Mexican history), on the one hand, and the dismissals of the future (i.e., the rejection of Mexican culture and identity by the West).

3.2. Cultural Nepantla

While nepantla is left unthematized (i.e., it does not become a theme of analysis itself) in the decades that follow Uranga's *Analysis*, it is certainly operative (working in the background as an assumed truth) in the work of Leopoldo Zea, Luis Villoro, and many other Mexican thinkers. It forcefully reemerges as theme of philosophical analysis almost fifty years later in Elsa Cecilia Frost's (1928–2005) "Acerca de Nepantla" ["On Nepantla"].[5] Here, Frost considers the dynamics of Mexican culture and argues that modern Mexican culture as a whole is, given its cultural and historical in-betweenness, a nepantla culture.

"On Nepantla" is Frost's inaugural address for the 14th Chair of the *Academy of the Mexican Letters*. Delivered less than a year before her death (November 11, 2004), "On Nepantla" proposes the idea—one grounded in history and archival records—that Mexican culture itself is "nepantla"—it is a *nepantla culture* (Frost 2018).

To begin with, Frost points out an "unease" prevalent among intellectuals in regard to the state of Mexican culture. This is an unease, or anxiety (*inquietud*), that begins in the aftermath of the Mexican Revolution of 1910. At that time, Mexican philosophers sought to figure out the state of Mexican culture after a war that quite nearly destroyed it. They ask about its nature and definition. In line with contemporary European and North American cultural theory, the standard approach was to classify Mexican culture as either "Latin American" (i.e., originally American) or "Iberian." Because Mexican culture retained aspects of both in its own way, both theorists and sociologists echoed the prominent view of Samuel Ramos, which said that Mexican culture was a "culture of imitation," that is, it was a bad copy of European culture. This verdict, Frost laments, "leaves this [the Mexican] portion of humanity in pretty bad standing."

Opposed to the standard approach, Frost suggests that while Mexican culture cannot be measured with any established cultural metrics, it is certainly *not* a culture of imitation, and the *struggle* to apply established cultural metrics simply means that it is "something quite distinct." The problem with those early evaluations of Mexican culture was, ultimately, that they accepted a Western standard of culture and of difference, failing to consider the possibility that Mexican culture did not have to be either European or originally American but something else (Frost 2018).

Examining the mid-sixteenth-century chronicles of Catholic missionaries, Frost suggests that while these set out to produce an "objective" history of the Conquest, the colony, and their own Christianizing efforts, something about the Mexican experience made this close to impossible. The missionaries themselves, for instance, could not make sense of *their own experience* in such an impersonal or objective way. Thus, in "*all* of the sixteenth century chronicles," Frost observes, a "characteristic passion" accompanied every account. It was as if life in Mexico could not be recounted by the evangelizers without, on the one hand, "shameless self-promotion," and on the other, a felt need to demean those to whom they ministered, to "denigrate their adversaries [the Indigenous peoples]" (Frost 2018; emphasis added).

The chronicles thus adopt a self-serving, subjective approach and in the process deny history its objectivity. Another way to say this is that what the chronicles reveal is a more accurate representation of *what Mexico meant* for the conquerors and not what it actually was. Moreover, no one in Europe could verify that what was pronounced as true or real was true or real. This gave the chroniclers the freedom to submerge themselves in their experience in an intimate and biased way until, eventually, the world that they were describing began to change them and they entered a process of nepantla. As nepantla, Frost says, the conquerors found themselves "conquered by their conquest" (2018).

What does it mean to say that the writers of the "last great theory of the West," as Frost describes the narrative of colonization and world-building created by New World historiography, were *conquered by their conquest*? Simply, it means that they began to *lose* themselves in their experience. And in this "losing of themselves" there emerged a crisis of identity, a loss of belonging, a loss of memory, and a loss of attachment to old ways of being. The Spanish began to experience a similar transition to what was being experienced by the indigenous peoples—a transition to an unknown and uncertain cultural future. By the time the Spanish friars and soldiers realized what was happening to them, the process of becoming *nepantla* had begun. The Spanish evangelizers began to experience the *never again* and *never yet* experience whereby one begins to feel nostalgia for both a past that will never be and a future that will never arrive. They began to lose their Spanishood.

Recalling Durán's account (cited earlier), Frost describes nepantla as a being "in the middle of the road . . . not fully Christian nor fully idolaters. Without fully belonging to either world." While Durán was angered by the indigenous man's attitude when confronted about his reckless spending, calling it an "abominable excuse" to hold on to pagan traditions, Frost recognizes the emancipatory tone of indigenous man's proclamation, one that announced a silent victory of the indigenous people over the Spanish "fathers": "the Indigenous man knew that he was better than Durán, who did not even know that *the Spanish were also nepantla*" (Frost 2018).

An interesting historical example of how the Spanish became nepantla has to do with food. On arrival, the Spanish refused to eat indigenous foods, but as time wore on, they grew accustomed to it, so long as they could use European spices to flavor the local dishes. Eventually, neither indigenous nor Spanish foods were consumed on their own, and their continued mixing eventually becomes a new cuisine, but one in constant process, in perpetual transition to becoming something else entirely.

According to Frost, this points to the origins of Mexican culture's recognition of itself as *neither Indigenous* (since that had been supplanted) *nor Spanish* (since this had done the supplanting), but as *something other*. This recognition motivates the search to find a concept that could capture this otherness, in the familiar vernacular of Western thinking. Here we see the origins of referring to Mexican culture as either "mestizo" and "criollo" (Frost 1972). However, these concepts prove to be overly rigid and fail at their purpose because they try to capture what is non-rigid, what is moving, in transit, always "in the middle"—an impossible task! Thus, Frost asks, "[c]ould we not apply nepantla to culture itself?" (Frost 2018).

A nepantla culture is a culture that is neither here nor there, neither this nor that, but always in transition, always fluid and dynamic, uncommitted to one or another determined way of life. In contemporary culture, Mexican American, Asian American, or Filipino American cultures are nepantla cultures.

I take Mexican American culture as an obvious example: it is conscious of itself as transitional, as always in the process of becoming "American" while never quite getting there; it unfolds in the middle of a historical inheritance (Mexico) and a promised ideal (the ideal of the "American way of life"); moreover, it knows itself as always moving further and farther away from its inheritance (linguistically, in the practice of cultural customs, in the naming of children, and so on).

According to Frost, nepantla is perfectly suited to capture not only the individual who lacks a firm ontological ground but a culture that can no longer affirm its own identity in a definite way. While the indigenous man who frustrates Durán with his spry remark may seem as though he expects to, one day, eventually, be fully what Durán wants him to be (he says, "*todavia estamos*," which means that they are *still being*, signifying that perhaps one day they will be other than what they currently are), Frost tells us that nepantla should be understood to refer, not to mestizaje, but to a "futureless hybridity," or a hybridity that will never come to fulfillment or be truly realized. Driving her point home, Frost (2018) writes:

> The colony was inhabited by Indians that no longer thought themselves as such and Spaniards who slowly ceased being so. Both different than their parents and, at the same time, creators of a new way of living that in the last instance is what we call culture.

In the end, it is Frost's remarkable way of appealing to colonial history that lends her philosophical pronouncements weight and significance. Nepantla is not only an abstract concept useful for the analysis of sixteenth-century Mexican culture, but a living concept that we find in the movement of culture itself, in its non-identity, yet traced back to the historical encounter between the West and its Other. Ultimately, we are authorized by Frost's observations to transpose the concept to our own time, applying it to the real life, flesh and bone, peoples, and cultures of the twenty-first century.

Finally, we recover and emphasize Frost's plot-twist: when the indigenous man says to Friar Durán "*we are still nepantla*," the "we" in "*todavia estamos*" refers to both the indigenous man *and* to Durán. Frost's insight that nepantla characterizes the colonizer as it does the colonized already problematizes the concept, making us see how nepantla can structure many different kinds of experiences. Hence, we can say that in our own day, nepantla captures not only those who have been defined in their in-betweenness by marginalization, colonialism, and intersectionality, but also those displaced by present circumstances, who in finding themselves in an ontological "no man's land" (even in the absence of recognized marginalization, colonialism, and intersectionality), find themselves out of sorts in-between time, worlds, and cultures (more on this later).

4. Nepantla as "*maña*"

For Durán, the being nepantla of the indigenous peoples signaled a type of social transformation that threatened the evangelizing program. It was a transformation that disguised itself as adaptation or assimilation: indigenous peoples dressing their ancient rituals in Christian garb so as to preserve them. Napantla was a mechanism of survival, a way to remain "neutral" and uncommitted to what was being proposed as a *new* way of existing. The indigenous peoples could hide behind this process as they undermined the projects of their Spanish conquerors. Even Durán observed:

> Incited by the devil . . . these miserable Indians remain perplexed and neutral regarding matters of faith . . . they believe in God and at the same time adore still their idols and appeal to their superstitions and ancient rituals, mixing one with the other. (quoted in Pérez 2011, 379)

Durán sees past the indigenous decolonial strategy, and while resorting to calling them "miserable" and "perplexed" [*perplejos*], knows them also as "*sutil y mañosos*," or "subtle and conniving" (379), as they "mix" in the old and the new so as to secretly preserve their ways.

Now, we can also translate "mañoso" as "cunning," but this is not the way that Durán means it. He is not happy with their strategy, so with "mañoso" he insinuates that the person is deceitful, sneaky, and one is advised to keep "an eye on" them as what they do is always self-serving and, we are advised, it is better not to fully trust them. A more positive understanding of "mañoso" is "cunning," suggesting that the person is crafty, wily, and has developed certain *habits* (*mañas*) that allow them to achieve certain ends in unorthodox or unfamiliar ways—you can count on these *mañosos* to get things done! This is not how Duráns means it.

Durán reads nepantla as a "maña" in a completely negative sense. This negative identification continues into postcolonial Mexico, to Latinx life in the United States, and to many others in our own time for whom nepantla is a contemporary mode of being human. "Mañosos" are thought to be unpredictable, unmanageable, and unwieldy, and so it is best to keep them marginalized and excluded.

In our discussion of nepantla, we understand it as a "maña" in a positive sense. It is a preservation strategy available to those existing as nepantla in between worlds, cultures, or catastrophes. Ultimately, nepantla is a way to preserve both a connection with the past and a certain kind of freedom in the present. Because one is neither here nor there, in-between, and so on, one can free oneself from present commitments and demands, from ties that nail one in place into a determinate way of being. Conceived in this positive way, a maña is certainly liberatory.

5. The Future of the Concept

In Mexican philosophy, being nepantla means that one exists in between fully articulated worlds, namely, the European and the indigenous. But it also means existing in between old and new, the beginning and the end, Spanish and Nahuatl, sense and nonsense, being and not being, coming and going, and life and death. The Aztecs described nepantla as "betwixt-and-betweenness … order-disorder, being-nonbeing, life-death … reciprocating balance … [where] human existence is defined by inescapable processing, becoming, and transformation" (Maffie 2015, 523).

Nepantla as transition or in-betweenness reveals a clear temporal dimension. Even historically, it names subjects suspended in what seems like a permanent moment of transition between a past that was once definitive and a future which never truly arrives. It has a *never again/yet never* structure: a temporal middlehood where one will *never again* be what one once was and, at the same time, a middlehood where the *yet to be* of the future will *never* arrive.

Now, the future of nepantla—however it may be deployed—depends on two factors. The first is recognizing the significance of its temporal dimension. This is especially the case for us, today. Inscribed in the linearity of contemporary forms of globalization is the idea that we can only move forward, which means a constant supplanting of the past and a constant sublation of tradition. Hence, in the age of globalization, we are *all* nepantla.

The second factor is related to the first, namely, that recognizing that we are all nepantla means that even those that do not understand themselves as nepantla are nepantla. Elsa Frost shows us that nepantla can also describe the colonizer, the oppressor, whose dependence on the colonized or oppressed means that they too are unsettled and in-between. This insight, however, means that nepantla is no longer solely a condition of the dispossessed, but also the dispossessor, who in a relation of dependence find themselves tied to the transitional destiny of the dispossessed and so seemingly always the middle of a profound change.

Phenomenologically speaking, we recognize nepantla most clearly in the experience of immigrants, exiles, or refugees, people who exist always "on the way," in between an origin to which they cannot return and a destination to which they may never arrive, one that may never offer them welcome, forcing them, then, to be "neutral" as to their commitments, "in the middle" as to their loyalties, and "in between" as to their being. This shows that nepantla applies broadly.

With this in mind, we can say that nepantla's depends on:

1. Our ability to see past the illusion of our own permanence, stability, and homogeneity and accept a kind of nomadism that assumes our being-always-on-the move but without hope of

arrival—in other words, it depends on our capacity to encounter our own inner immigrant and accept it;

2. That we recognize nepantla as describing culture itself.

Applying nepantla to culture means that it not only describes those for whom hybridity is a historical reality, including all marginalized and historically oppressed peoples, but all who find themselves in-between times, spaces, or dimensions of existence. That is, nepantla can be applied to cultures that find themselves in-between, in the middle, or suspended in its transitions among the way things used to be and their historical trajectory.

In its original sense, nepantla referred to a past that was lost through an expropriation, through colonization, via cultural oppressions, which could be subtle or explicit, or through some other sort of systemic or symbolic violence; this meant that the lack of one's foothold in the *never again* and the *never yet* was ultimately a result of the intersection of these and many other oppressions.

According to Uranga, nepantla describes Mexican being in its in-between worlds, to wit, the indigenous and Spanish worlds; it describes Mexican being as "in the middle" of a seemingly endless journey, always in transit, migrating and immigrating always further away from its indigenous roots and toward a European lifeworld to which it is destined never to fully arrive; and, Mexican being is nepantla in being neutral in response to claims made on its identity by others, on the one hand, or by its own conscience, on the other—in nepantla, that is, Mexican being suspends its allegiances to whatever seeks to define it rigidly as either this or that.

What I am proposing now is that nepantla will describe a general, phenomenologically and historically obvious, being in the middle, a perpetual transition, which is both inescapable and irrevocable. This expands the notion substantially. Thus, in our own time, we can understand nepantla as an ontological/existential category referring to being *out of place, out of time,* and, even, *out of self.* Again, take the plight of Mexican Americans as one example. One is out of place in not properly identifying with North American history, on the one hand, nor with Mexican history, one the other. One is out of time in being historically orphaned by both, a phenomenon that explains an attitude of neutrality toward or abstention from ideals essential to the first, for instance, ideals of American individualism or mass consumption, or essential to the second, for instance, Mexicans ideal of masculinity or family.

Zozobra

(so-so-brah)

Overview of the Concept: *Zozobra names the feeling of doom, desperation, or uncertainty that defines modern life. We can fall into or be consumed by it, just like we can fall into or be consumed by joy or the fear of death. Unlike the experience of being consumed by or falling into joy, however, in zozobra we are delivered over to a version of the world (which is* our *version of the world) in crisis—a divided, unsettled world. This world appears at once as a familiar and unfamiliar, one that we easily recognize but which nonetheless feels uncanny and strangely weird. We find ourselves certain of two things simultaneously: that this is our world and that this is not our world. This is a contradiction essential to zozobra, and it filters our experience in such a way that we don't know what to believe, what to depend on. Perhaps by accident or perhaps by necessity, zozobra is our condition. Moreover, in zozobra we are overcome not only by uncertainty, unsettledness, and disquiet but also by an engulfing sense of sentimentality, a kind of all-consuming mourning for a world that suddenly appears lost and unrecoverable. In zozobra, existing truly feels strange and uncomfortable.*

The Covid-19 pandemic of 2020 stopped us in our tracks. Suddenly, we were sheltered in our homes, fearing for our lives, uncertain about a future that moments before appeared to open itself out into an ordered and anticipated tomorrow. Political, racial, and economic crises soon followed the global "lockdown"; we found ourselves in the shadow of the radically unfamiliar and, as the pandemic extended into new seasons, our crisis became catastrophic.

The breakdown of familiar routines availed us the realization that perhaps we had previously been living *as if* certainty and stability were the default state of existence. Of course, our contemporary metanarratives make room for uncertainty and unpredictability. But now, and as the pandemic raged on and living itself became more and more precarious, the uncertainty inscribed in our pre-pandemic worldview seemed like a luxury, something to counter-balance the order and stability regulating modern life. This *new* uncertainty, however, was nowhere inscribed; it did not fit our expectations on what uncertainty was supposed to be, it was unstable, disruptive, and scary. As the pandemic became the norm, uncertainty turned into panic as we imagined our own ruin always one breath away. Apocalyptic mass media prophets warned that this catastrophe was perhaps something we were not equipped to handle, that it was, perhaps, not something we would survive. We were offered a frightening picture of our very next moment; even the illusory stability offered by modern technology was torn to shreds. The constant bombardment of fatalism fed our dread and broke down our defenses. The rug was been pulled out from under our feet, and the floor beneath revealed as quicksand. Uncertainty became desperation. In Mexican philosophy, the name for this *feeling* of sinking, desperation, and uncertainty is "zozobra."

Students of European existential philosophy will seek to name our contemporary feeling of sinking or uncertainty with established Western concepts like "anxiety," "angst," and "nausea"; it is the "dizziness of freedom" (Kierkegaard 1981), a "mood" of indeterminate dread in the face of one's "being-toward-death" (Heidegger 1962, Div II, ch. 6), and the disgust one feels at confronting our place amid bare, naked, being (Sartre 2005). Anxiety, angst, and nausea already track the existential feeling of being abandoned by certainty or alienated from the sources of meaning.[1] However, what distinguishes zozobra from its European counterparts, a difference which is subtle but significant, is that while zozobra places us before the fact of our thrownness and with the sheer contingency of our own existence, it *also* delivers us over into an emotionally charged confrontation with *extreme* and *contradictory* possibilities of being, into a world and an existence where our choices threaten to tear us in two.

In short, we can say that in zozobra we are delivered over to a version of the world (*our* version of the world) in crisis. It appears at once as a familiar and unfamiliar world, one that we've always known but which *now* feels uncanny and weirdly other. We feel certain of two things simultaneously: this is our world and this is not our world. This is a contradiction essential to zozobra, and it filters our experience in such a way that we don't know what to believe, what to depend on, and so it is and it is not our world, simultaneously. Perhaps by accident or perhaps by necessity, we are in it. We are overcome not only by uncertainty, unsettledness, and disquiet but also by an overwhelming sense of sentimentality, a kind of mourning for a world that suddenly seems lost and unrecoverable. We are in zozobra and existence feels strange.

Consequently, as picking out a complex and contradictory attitude toward a world in crisis, zozobra fits right into an analytical arsenal that may help us make sense of the confrontation with contingency, indeterminacy, and uncertainty common to modern life. It is my view that zozobra tracks the heterogeneity of contemporary existence more closely than other concepts in the Western canon. This chapter is an invitation to include zozobra in the register of (teachable) philosophical concepts and, by extension, lend credence to the value of Mexican philosophy as a resource for making sense of our world.

Understanding zozobra requires us to recognize it as emerging from the Mexican intellectual tradition. In what follows, my focus is on its articulation by Emilio Uranga.

1. Zozobra in Mexican Philosophy

The concept "zozobra" is not of Mexican origin. It is a Spanish term with Latin roots (sub + supra/under + over) referring in particular to nautical events, for instance, dangerous sailing conditions or the act of a boat capsizing.[2] While it shows up in philosophical treatments of human existence, significantly in the work of the Spanish philosopher José Ortega y Gasset (2009) who uses it to refer to a state of being tormented by loss and abandonment,[3] the concept is otherwise left unthematized or untreated in his philosophy. It is with Mexican philosophers that zozobra finds its *philosophical* treatment. While it can be translated in its most straightforward sense as "distress,"[4] "anxiety," "disquiet," or even "disenchantment," I have chosen to leave it untranslated for two reasons: one, for the sake of preserving philosophical difference, and two, for the simple reason that when treated philosophically, it encompasses all of these different existential and psychic modalities and more.

In Mexican philosophy, zozobra becomes the central theme in Emilio Uranga's 1949 essay "Essay on the Ontology of the Mexican" (2017) and, again, a few years later, in 1952, in his seminal, *Analysis of Mexican Being* (2021). Seeking to give a name to the restless discontent and uncertainty of post-Revolutionary life almost three decades after the conclusion of revolutionary hostilities, Uranga arrives at "zozobra," a term he appropriates, not from any Western sources, but from the poetry of the Mexican poet, Ramón López Velarde (1888-1921).

While Velarde does not treat the concept in any great detail, his poetry seeks to capture it. In fact, it is the name of one of Velarde's most celebrated collections, published in 1919. The poems included in Velarde's *Zozobra* treat of mourning, of loss, of unending suffering; at the same time, however, these are poems about longing, love, and hope. Written in the aftermath of Velarde's lover's death, and toward the end of the Mexican Revolution, the poems evoke the hopelessness and sentimentality that overcome individuals, societies, and peoples, who are rudderless, groundless, and lacking any certainties on which to anchor their future (Velarde 1919).

Uranga thinks that in Velarde's poetry one can find, he says, "all the 'elements' of our character" (Uranga 2021, 168). According to Uranga, Velarde succeeds in capturing an atmosphere with poetry that is at once a reflection of loss and hope in the shadow of catastrophe (the Revolution and the death of his lover) and, according to Uranga, an accurate picture of a historical identity which is accidental and sentimental.

1.1 *The Logic of Zozobra*

Velarde is Uranga's most significant philosophical inspiration. He reads Velarde's *Zozobra* as the testimony of the post-Revolutionary Mexican experience and reinterprets that experience with phenomenological intent, finding, beyond the contingencies of the poetry, an essential nucleus that had previously authorized Velarde to *name* an entire poetic and existential orientation. Attending thus to the poetry, Uranga arrives at a restlessness and despair that captures a feeling, and a state, that's all too familiar: one belonging to his own circumstance and his own people.

The truth of zozobra (and *Zozobra*), however, will not speak only to and about Mexicans. Uranga locates it as characteristic of that which is accidental; he says it is "the abandoned inspiration of accidentality" (Uranga 2021, 170–1). By this, Uranga means that zozobra is tied to the pathos of the accident, that it is part of the sentimentality that propels it. This also means that zozobra is a characteristic of non-Mexican others, and in particular, of "those others that through a thousand accidents of history, of culture or society, have been framed by the catastrophic" (187).

The "others" to which Uranga refers are those whose histories and cultures have been "framed" by violence, colonialism, and empire— that is, the "catastrophic." And these are many. Because catastrophism can ensnare us all (through colonialism or pandemic, for instance), we can say that Uranga's analysis of zozobra (and his philosophy more generally) addresses a more expansive community. Uranga allows for this reading, as he defines zozobra in a way that is applicable to anyone likewise "framed" by history.

We arrive at a general definition:

Zozobra refers to a mode of being that incessantly oscillates between two possibilities, between two affects, without knowing on which one of those to depend . . . indiscriminately dismissing one extreme in favor of the other. In this to and fro the soul suffers, it feels torn and wounded. The pain of zozobra is not obviously identifiable with fear or anxiety, it takes from both in an emotionally ambiguous manner. (Uranga 2021, 180)

This overarching definition seeks to capture zozobra's existential structure as a *state* and a *feeling*: as a state, it is "mode of being," an incessant oscillation between "affects" and other "extremes"; as a feeling, it is an emotive in-betweenness which is also other to fear and anxiety.

On an abstract, or better yet, global level, zozobra describes human being as frantically oscillating between extreme possibilities of existence, all of which are the only possibilities available and none of which are conducive to feeling optimistic about one's fortunes, nor promising any sort of tranquility. In other words, this in-betweenness is not a mere suspension between extremes (this is *nepantla*, see Chapter 2); the in-betweenness of zozobra is pendular, oscillating, frenzied, and desperate. Uranga says that "the coming and going has no end" (167–8) and that the "soul suffers" as it commits itself to its "pendular" existence (168), and its "catastrophism" (185). To be in zozobra is thus to exist *in* and *as* oscillation and *as* oscillation between extremes which are extreme, insecure, uncertain, or violent.

This existing-in excessive pendularity reflects a living *with* or in the shadow of catastrophe, a place from where the world always appears as if on the brink of collapse, implosion, or ruin. In such a state, one becomes accustomed to, or dependent on, the consistency of contradiction and unsettledness. Among friends or acquaintances, we are prone to express this being-accustomed as a resigned "it is the way it is." Moreover, this being-accustomed to zozobra means that living between extremes has become ordinary, and a life *without* contradiction, insecurity, and uncertainty unimaginable; in such a state, one "settles" into zozobra as it becomes impossible to think oneself without it or beyond it—this an unsettled settling.

Hence, Uranga suggests that while in zozobra one becomes accustomed to "simultaneously depend on . . . extremes [and] to not let go [*no soltar presa*], to hold on to both ends of the chain" (Uranga 2021, 167). The image that this evokes, that of "holding on to both ends of the chain," recalls another: that of the grisly medieval practice of quartering, whereby a person is brutally dismembered by tying each of the four limbs to horses going in opposite directions. Zozobra is not unlike a being quartered, but instead of horses, life's urgent and contradictory demands, and instead of being tied to those demands, one obstinately holds on to them, unable to let go despite the threat of being torn to pieces.

It is clearly irrational to be obstinate in this way, holding on to ropes that will tear one apart, yet this further illustrates zozobra's internal logic. Zozobra's logic is a different sort of logic; for sure, it does not conform to "Western" logic. The logic of zozobra is such that contradiction does not, in fact, cancel anything out; two options that would otherwise annul each other can remain in play simultaneously, and I can hold on to equally opposing positions, which are equally irrational, and contradictory, and harmful to myself. In zozobra, holding on to the ropes that will tear me apart (i.e., being-accustomed) has the same "logical" force as letting them go. Uranga puts it this way:

> [Zozobra's peculiar ontological movement] does not correspond either to a linear formal logic or to spiral dialectical logic. Contradictory terms exclude themselves in a formal logic, and in order to construct an image of a justifiable character, one must reject one of the terms in order to preserve the other. In a dialectic, both extremes are overcome and are synthesized so as to give birth to a third moment that will absorb the contraries, sublimating them perfectly in a new term. (Uranga 2021, 167)

Uranga calls this "the logic of oscillation." In accordance with this logic, zozobra does not abide by the constraints of Eurocentric logic or Eurocentric ways of making sense of the world; it conforms neither to the linearity of the syllogism (simply: if A is B, and B is C, therefore, A is C) nor to the law of excluded middle (simply: a proposition cannot be both true and false at the same time) nor to dialectical logic (simply: X, the negation of X, the negation of the negation of X, which is a new X). Zozobra's logic is the logic of randomness and accident, refusing form and linearity, dialectic and synthesis, taking the form of "perhaps," "certainly," "never," "always," "yes or no," and "yes and no" (P and not-P). Uranga describes this logic as an accumulation and a "not letting go" of extremes. Ultimately, this "rocking to and fro, the coming and going" of zozobra characterizes the transitional, that is, the temporal structure of human being as accident.[5]

We can illustrate this logic by thinking about simultaneously loving *and* hating a person. Against the dictates of "linear formal logic," in zozobra one can do both at the same time; the law of excluded middle does not apply as one cannot let go of either the love or the hate, fully committing oneself to both. Neither is a synthesis produced as in "dialectical logic"—overtaken by zozobra, one does not arrive at, for instance, tolerance, as the happy medium of the two emotions. In zozobra one oscillates between loving and hating that person, at times doing both at once, unable to let go of the love or the hate, and knowing that these are the only possibilities. Naturally, as Uranga points out, the "soul feels wounded" as it struggles, and fails, to create a new situation out of them.

The metaphor of being quartered or the example of loving and hating a person refers to the idea that the responsibility for one's suffering ultimately falls on oneself since it is I who does not let go, it is my ego which holds on to contradiction and incoherence; with this, we may conclude that there is no escape, or relief, from zozobra's logical traps. However, Uranga hints at a way out, namely, a way to look beyond oneself in the *hope* and expectation of community. Even in the torment of not knowing what future to depend on, of obstinately depending on contradictory and extreme options for living, of frantically moving from one possibility to another, there remains hope for an "encounter" with others likewise tormented or wounded.

1.2 *Forging Ourselves as Zozobra*

Existence remains suspended between two abysses—one of misery, one of infinity—thus keeping itself in suspense about itself. Instability is its permanent condition, uncertainty its natural state. Perpetually oscillating between extremes and unattainable situations, man travels on, unable to steady himself, fearful and trembling. In fear and trembling, yes . . . but, also, in *faith* and *hope*? (Villoro 2017, 155)

When I am gripped, or seized, by zozobra, "uncertainty" becomes my "natural state." In this state, "existence" itself is "suspended between two abysses": one is "misery," the other "infinity." These seem like the only options. I find it hard to choose between misery and infinity since the former is the facticity that I know while the latter is the absolutely other—the unknown. It's a choice between life and death. Like Hamlet, I do not know which is better. I sink deeper into uncertainty. In fear and trembling, I suffer my slow death by quartering. In spite of feeling like I'm being torn apart, I hold on without relaxing my grip. This is tiring.

Zozobra is exhausting. I am exhausted in both senses of this term: I feel tired and emptied. Tired of being stretched by conflicting demands, tired of the to and fro, and tired of the uncertainty, but also empty of options and wanting of peace and tranquility. It is from that place of want and exhaustion, however, that zozobra reveals *itself* as the opportunity for surrender.

Surrendering to the indecision does not mean one has overcome the fear and trembling of zozobra before the "abyss," but Villoro suggests that a new possibility may open up, the possibility of "faith and hope" amid uncertainty. Actualizing this possibility, however, means, Uranga says, that we must "forge our character as zozobra."

To forge our character as zozobra . . . is an invocation or incitation. It is to gather oneself in an alveolus in an attitude of expectation. The hollow space in which the ground of randomness has been prepared is somewhat somber, cavernous; one cannot say that it is an opening bathed in light. It is chiaroscuro, twilight, "penumbra." But attention shines in the depths of that cave, as does hope, the vigil of the prayerful

. . . Hearts that are punished and in zozobra lie in a gloomy hollow, but there they are alert. Here we note the combination of darkness and light. To submerge oneself in originary zozobra seems to be a movement that brings us closer to darkness, toward the annulment of consciousness. But at that extreme point when we are about to give ourselves over to twilight, our wakefulness shines, a subtle antenna readies to receive the message. (Uranga 2021, 172–3)

Forging our character as zozobra means that one no longer trembles in fear before the abyss. Perhaps one releases one's grip on the ropes, letting the horses pull one apart without resisting. Uranga says that this would be to "gather oneself in an alveolus in . . . expectation." Because the alveoli are tiny air pockets in the lungs that replenish oxygen in the human body, the metaphor here suggests that to forge ourselves as zozobra, and thus to surrender to its chaotic logic, is to *expect* zozobra to replenish us in some way—to have faith that zozobra will save us or heal us. The process will not be painless, as this place of expectation and faith is not "bathed in light," meaning that we may be quartered after all; however, as we give ourselves over to zozobra, we also become "alert," "prayerful" and *hopeful*—because, what else is prayer but articulated hope?

Our reading suggests that the temporality of zozobra (its duration) is no match for hope, which in the "gloomy hollow" of the alveolus, emerges as an expectation for an end and the arrival of something other. In other words, giving myself over to zozobra, or submerging myself in it, means that I am ready to see it through to the end. This end comes as zozobra takes me "closer to darkness" and, closer still, to the "annulment of consciousness," that is, to the end of my quartering, that is, to the edge of infinity or my own death. Hope emerges when zozobra ends, when, Uranga says, "wakefulness shines." This wakefulness is the suspension, or delaying, of death together with the revelation of an encounter with something greater, perhaps a community of similarly afflicted, perhaps God. Whatever it may be, my "antenna readies to receive the message."

Submersion in zozobra, or forging ourselves as zozobra, is thus the only way to survive it, exhausting and frightening as this submergence may be. This is possible, moreover, because "zozobra," Uranga continues, "is not an enclosed pool, but an open channel" (185). Surrendering to zozobra thus opens us up to a possibility that in resistance we could not see. As an open channel, zozobra itself promises an escape from my solitude into that community of random tributaries, at once uncertain in their flow, at once determined by the unforgiving terrain, but always flowing to the meeting place, to community and communication.

1.3 *Zozobra and Community*

It is hard to imagine what surrendering to zozobra *looks* like. Uranga's ontological commitments make it so that it is difficult to translate what *gathering oneself in an attitude of expectation* means in everyday life. If this is a possibility for being, could then this not also be a possibility for me? In the terror and misery of indecision and uncertainty, in zozobra, I accept my place and I surrender to the thought that any of my choices will kill me. In surrender, I "gather" myself in an "attitude of expectation," that is, in an attitude of *hope*. What do I hope for? I hope that what I feel now will end, or, even, that I am not the only one terrified and miserable in this way. Ultimately, I've surrendered to the thought that I am not alone. I must find the others.

Uranga (2021) says cryptically: "In this pendular movement [of Zozobra] there is a passive synthesis, a fulfillment of things brought about through . . . heterogeneous encounters" (168). The suggestion here is that random encounters with others likewise gripped by zozobra will steady the frenzied and terrifying logic of zozobra in each one of us, namely, via "a passive synthesis." My need for others grows as I recognize that my individual struggle need not be mine alone. This unanticipated recognition of other zozobras creates a *hope* for community of "heterogeneous" individuals who may contribute to a steadying of my inner life; one does not need to go it alone.

This is what it means for zozobra to be an "open channel" that delivers us to a meeting place, to a confluence or convergence where others await in sympathy and understanding. Our journey to a zozobra community will be rough, and we will weather contradictions, torment, and uncertainty; but without our zozobra, the hope itself will not have been possible. For this reason Uranga (2021) audaciously claims that zozobra makes "communication possible" allowing "creatures of all kinds communicate one with the other" (171). In other words, as we encounter communities of those similarly affected by catastrophism and zozobra, we will have something to share. Zozobra makes communication possible because it allows us to authentically connect with one another from a space of vulnerability and suffering.

In a way, zozobra transforms our vision, allowing us to see one another in our trauma, thus it is capable of connecting us with strangers across time and space. Even if random and isolated, our otherwise private zozobra will be familiar to others, if not in content (the strength of the horses that will tear me apart), then in form (the quartering), and so it can be "seen" in what we say and how we say it.

The *hope* internal to zozobra is that we will, in time, converge with others in spaces of empathy or sympathy, similarly to "the vertical fall of atoms [in the Epicurean universe which] have to endure an inflexion so that their encounter comes about" (171). The result of this convergence is community and togetherness, a space of communicative action and dialogue, a space for the sharing of individual experiences and trauma. For these reasons, Uranga writes that "in zozobra we find foundational moments in the formation of intersubjectivity, with all of its modalities" (180).

We thus imagine persons of different cultural backgrounds brought together by historical accidents and random circumstances. While their togetherness is accidental, while it lacks predetermination, a fixed direction, or purpose, they will seek to share their suffering and the catastrophe that defines their experience, one that despite particular differences, can serve as the point of departure for any type of intersubjective interchange, cooperation, sympathy, caring, or creating. This means that one must know one's zozobra, and know it intimately, just in case one comes across an opportunity to share it.

1.4 *The Names of Zozobra*

The preceding shows that zozobra is *not* identical to its dictionary—pre-theoretical—definition. The standard definition of "zozobra," which follows its colloquial use, is that zozobra is "uneasiness, anguish, or anxiety." And, minimally, it is. But, as Uranga (2021) points out, "[t]he pain of zozobra is not obviously identifiable with fear or anxiety; it takes from both in an emotionally ambiguous manner" (180). What does this mean? Crucially, it means that zozobra is not straightforwardly fear or anxiety, unease, or anguish; it is essentially all of these and more.

We can say that zozobra borrows from the gamut of emotional states (fear, anxiety, unease, etc.) in such a way that it is not clear what it is that we are feeling when possessed by it. As our minds oscillate between possibilities of existence we become emotionally unsettled, a phenomenon that tracks existence in a most general sense. This leads Uranga to say that zozobra characterizes the emotive being of human beings in a foundational way. He thus broadens the definition beyond its colloquial use by having it refer to more foundational emotional states of being as well as to those psychological, feeling, states that are familiar and that may seem more superficial.

Table 3.1 highlights the different ways in which Uranga characterizes zozobra, an apparent terminological indecisiveness that points to zozobra's essential indeterminateness.

This list is not exhaustive. It does show, however, that zozobra is much more than isolated moments of anxiety, anguish, angst, nausea, or dread. It refers to a full emotive experience, one that opens us up, ultimately, to a surrender from which one can see beyond our current misery and to, perhaps, the hope offered by community. These diverse characterizations also reveal zozobra, moreover, as a foundational emotive condition which, although *foundational*, is never static or inert; *like* nepantla, it is thus *not a mere* suspension between its extremes (see previous chapter).[6]

To be sure, anxiety, angst, and nausea are still available as terms we can use to describe our condition; however, these have taken on

Table 3.1 Characterizations of Zozobra © Carlos Alberto Sánchez

	Relevant Passage
Sentimentality	"[Zozobra] does not oscillate inside an obscure and empty space, but rather, the space is colored, or painted, with a sentimental atmosphere. That is why we have said that more than a movement of will, zozobra is an emotive to and fro, it is sentimental" (Uranga 2021, 174).
Uncertainty	"[Z]ozobra is a 'not knowing what to depend on'" (167).
Foreboding	"Zozobra is the state in which we are not sure, if at any moment, a catastrophe will overwhelm us or if we will be secure in the safety of asylum" (173).
Unsettledness	"The incessant rocking to and fro, the coming and going, has no end; we could say with López Velarde (who will always have the last word in our ontology) that 'our lives are pendulums'" (67–168).
Obstinacy	Zozobra is "to simultaneously depend on both extremes, to accumulate, to not let go [*no soltar presa*], to hold on to both ends of the chain" (167).
Indecisiveness	"In zozobra we remain in suspense, in oscillation" (173).
Disquiet	Zozobra is "a spiritual state that is nothing close to tranquility" (181).
Oscillation	"What we say about the logic of oscillation corresponds to what we may say about zozobra. This peculiar ontological movement that is zozobra does not correspond either to a linear formal logic or to spiral dialectical logic. Contradictory terms exclude themselves in a formal logic, and in order to construct an image of a justifiable character, one must reject one of the terms in order to preserve the other. In a dialectic, both extremes are overcome and are synthesized so as to give birth to a third moment that will absorb the contraries, sublimating them perfectly in a new term" (167).
Restlessness	"We must always know what we can count on, but the belief that we can never know what we can count on constitutes our restlessness or zozobra" (Uranga 2017, 173).

Table 3.1 (Continued)

	Relevant Passage
Randomness	Zozobra "is the abandoned inspiration of accidentality" and "randomness," that is, "what is hybrid, the pairing of incompatible kinds, of contradictory kinds . . . it is the crooked furrow that in a sudden crisscross brings together the heterogeneous, connecting the specific and particular in a rigid definition" (Uranga 2021, 170–1).
Vulnerability	"We are at the mercy of whatever may come, we are constitutively fragile" (Uranga 2017, 173).
A foundational schema	"What must be kept in mind as decisive is not, I insist, the content, but the schema, one that we preliminarily refer to as logical, pendular, oscillating, and zigzagging. In a word: zozobra" (Uranga 2021, 167).
The possibility of communication	"[Z]ozobra is nothing else but the naked skeleton of that universal to and fro that allows creatures of all kinds to communicate one with the other" (171).
A possibility for understanding	"To submerge oneself in originary zozobra seems to be a movement that brings us closer to darkness, toward the annulment of consciousness. But, at the extreme point when we are about to give ourselves over to twilight, our wakefulness shines" (172).
Passive synthesis	"In this pendular movement there is a passive synthesis, a fulfillment of things brought about through the sorrowful chance of heterogeneous encounters" (168).
An open channel	"In zozobra we find foundational moments in the formation of intersubjectivity, with all of its modalities" (180).

their own, restricted meaning both in the history of philosophy and in everyday life. Moreover, there are treatments for these conditions because they have been reduced to some physiological or psychological *dis-ease* that can be addressed with chemicals, therapy, prayer, or meditation—or all four together. No such cure or treatment exists for zozobra.

2. Zozobra in the Time of Pandemic

These days, economic insecurity, political upheaval, the threat of climate catastrophe, and the mere speed of modern life threaten to topple our sails, making us feel as though we're capsizing. This feeling is zozobra, and it seems to be the default setting for contemporary living, revealing us overrun with uncertainty, contradiction, and foreboding, but also, and in a vague and irrational way, as obstinate accomplices to our own self-destruction. Here, we recall that zozobra does not conform to Western logics, that it is a holding on to contradictory extremes without "knowing what to depend on," or equally, "to simultaneously depend on both" and "to not let go [*no soltar presa*], to hold on to both ends of the chain" (Uranga 2021, 167).

Among our modern catastrophes, pandemic is the most recent.

For many of us, the possibility of a global pandemic had been unthinkable. Finding ourselves unexpectedly in one, we did not know what to make of it or how to articulate it to ourselves or others. Suddenly, and without warning, we were thrust into our solitude; peeking out of windows, we became nostalgic for pre-pandemic sociality and became concerned about some future "new normal." We also wondered if the "silent killer" was lurking outside our front door. As the days lost their distinctiveness, a nostalgic disconnection from others defined the nature of our solitude. This specific sort of solitude was a mixture of alienation, longing, and fear that, mixed with powerlessness and uncertainty, fearfully kept us separated from one another. Yet, fearful and uncertain, we nonetheless longed for conviviality and community with people—with those we knew and with those with which we had never interacted. We zig-zagged from paranoia to nostalgia to terror, meanwhile wanting to intermingle with those whose breath we imagined would kill us.

Different possibilities, each prophesizing our doom, presented themselves at once. We longed to be with others, and, perhaps, dying as a result. We found ourselves trapped in between extremes, neither of which we felt was avoidable and both to which we stubbornly clung. On one extreme, our paranoid fear of a slow, anonymous, death that waited for us outside our doorstep; this pulled us inward, deeper into despair and unsettledness. On the other, a sentimental longing for being with others, for company, and community; this pulled us outward, but further into our suffering. But we could not just be afraid and we could not just be nostalgic; we were both at once, and this only prolonged our zozobra, and with that our exhaustion.

While it is imprecise to say that zozobra is a ground of existence since it is a frenzied moving to and fro, it is nonetheless grounding. However, it is not the kind of ground in which we can settle into: "this ground is not a fixed and firm foundation, but rather it is unstable quicksand upon which nothing firm can stand" (Uranga, 181). And so we feel restless, unbalanced, and uncertain about our footing. In the immediacy of the moment, forging our character as zozobra is not an option as we don't know what to believe. We are without hope. Disquiet sets in. "To constantly refer to that region in which possibilities face and confront themselves creates a spiritual state that is nothing close to tranquility" (181). According to its "logic," moreover, being in zozobra also means that a synthesis of fear and nostalgia will not settle us. We will not suddenly be *at peace* with our situation, and we will continue to hold on to both extremes, to both ends of the chain, and remain in between, restlessly trying to reconcile that which is tearing us in two, or four.

But all is not lost. As a zozobra-inducing catastrophe, the Coronavirus pandemic placed us on the path to surrender; it created the conditions for the possibility of a submersion into our own zozobra, it created the condition for the possibility of surrender; once surrendered, we could then wait for the opening to something beyond. That space of surrender, moreover, what Uranga metaphorically calls an "alveolus," is a place of quiet and stillness and, in stillness, hope. At one point, Uranga (2021) defines "hope" as "the vigil of the prayerful" (172), meaning that hope is an expectation for the faithful. But not just any expectation. It is the expectation of a zozobra-less future. In times of catastrophe, our vigil is all that we have; in times of pandemic, our salvation *feels* as if it's coming in the form of a cure, from immunity, or from a miracle. This *feeling* points simultaneously back to a moment of surrender and immediately to our hope.

While this talk of hope in the midst of what seems like a hopelessness situation may sound ambiguous and contradictory, we recall that the logic of zozobra allows for such ambiguity and contradiction. Its logic is nonlinear and inconsistent, we can be fearful of others and longing for others at the same time, or at once afraid and not afraid of others. This is the source of anxiety and disquiet, but also the source of hope, since hope is likewise (according to its logic) not excluded from its possibility. The faith and hope that comes from the terror of submitting to the thought that we may all be consumed by pandemic (i.e., our surrendering to zozobra) is not prohibited to any of us, but especially to those of us who live *in* this logic; to those of us whose "lives are pendulums."[7]

3. Zozobra and Surrender

Zozobra is complex. In it, one is overcome with sentimentality and obstinacy, foreboding and disquiet, all the while oscillating between extremes and contradictions. However, being overwhelmed by it also affords one the possibility of surrender, and with surrender, something beyond—hope. When we "forge ourselves as zozobra," when we allow it to be, or surrender to it, we suspend our struggle with it; in doing so, it delivers us to a beyond, to what answers the prayers of the hopeful. This beyond is community, a place of gathering and confluence, where the suffering meets and communicates. Zozobra connects us with one another's inner torment. This connection, unintentional and passive, which is created in the background of our doings, is the source of hope.

In this way, and despite ontological commitments that would otherwise not allow normative claims to be made, Uranga lends zozobra a constitutive role in the formation of community and sociality. Thus, while something like anxiety can isolate the individual in an existential solitude (a being-alone with your anxiety), zozobra makes community possible (a tending toward others). It does this by being a kind of permanent internal suffering that we seek to expunge, that we seek to externalize, by singing about it or writing about it, lending it a visible profile. We also recognize it in others, in what they do and what they say. We are all witnesses to one another's dismemberment. And in this state we meet.

Ultimately, zozobra does not just put me before the fact of my own existence, what existentialists call my *facticity*, but before my facticity in crisis. In this crisis, I am confronted with contradictory versions of my present, all excessive, unsettling, and terrifying. Despite this crisis, however, despite the constant and persistent feeling of capsizing and drowning, foreboding and obstinacy, a vague hope remains, and with it a kind of tranquility that on the far side of these extremes I will find others.

Of course, there is a danger to this being-open-to-community that zozobra makes possible. For instance, vulnerable from the ravages of zozobra's contradictions and oscillations, from zozobra's quarterings, one can awaken into a destructive community, such as those overtaken by the nihilistic impulse of *relajo* (see Chapter 1).

4

Corazonadas

(core-asohn-ad-as)

Overview of the Concept: *A "corazonada" (also translated as "intimation") refers to an experience of certainty rooted in the immediacy of an emotional/affective encounter or immersion with a determinate or familiar state of affairs. Less abstractly, a corazonada lets you "know," immediately and without rationalizations, that something is the case; you just feel it to be true or right because it can't be otherwise than true or right (or false and wrong). One uses phrases like "it just hit me" or "I know it when I see it," where "it" refers to an aspect of circumstantial reality, a truth, a thought, or an insight, to characterize the experience. It is not an intuition or a gut feeling but something like a heart-knowing.*

My work on Mexican philosophy has focused on that singular moment in the middle of the twentieth century when Mexican philosophy asked into the *being of the Mexican*. What I have discovered is that while philosophical answers to questions regarding national, historical, and cultural identity always assume that "something" about "the Mexican" is readily given, these answers also assume that there are *facts* that, if not scientific, are at least plainly observable in language, in the arts, music, traditions, customs, and so on. However, "facts" that answer the "ontological question" about "Mexican being" are not given in this way. Epistemic instruments like perception or rational intuition fall short of arriving at "what it is like" *to be* Mexican. To this end, Emilio Uranga (2021) proposes what he calls "*corazonadas ontológicas*," which, according to Uranga, offer an affective, and effective, access to the sort of evidence required for the ontological characterization of Mexican being.

The affective nature of corazonadas ontológicas can be gathered from the etymology of "corazonada." At its root, the Spanish term "corazonada" derives from the word "corazón," meaning "heart." This suggests that the heart, and not the mind, is a privileged source of or access to justification, truth, or revelation. The Spanish word itself is technically defined in dictionaries as "presentiment," "foreboding," and the "courage, or impulse of the heart to encounter dangers" (Vazquez 2005, 298). On this definition, a literal translation into English of "corazonada" is "hunch," "gut feeling," or "intimation." Translating it as "hunch," "courage," or "gut feeling," however, seems to place too much emphasis on some kind of predictive knowledge of *things to come*. This seems to rob it of its philosophical weight, since what Uranga means by it is closer to a sort of *confident knowing*, which is not clear that hunches, courage, or gut feelings give us (we'll come back to gut feelings later). Elsewhere, I've thus translated it as "intimation" (Uranga 2021), since the English word "intimation" retains that aspect of a confident knowing central to what Uranga has in mind.[1] While in what follows we leave it in its Spanish original, the reader is invited to read "intimation" in its place whenever appropriate.

The notion of corazonada is introduced into Mexican philosophy by the Spanish philosopher and "transterrado"[2] Juan-David García Bacca (1901–92), who, while reflecting on the eternal Don Quixote, identifies the corazonada that thrusts Don Quixote into action, one reflected in his passionate, and impulsive, love for the maiden Dulcinea.

In this context, Bacca goes on to define "corazonada" as follows: "*Corazonada is the correspondence of a sentimental shock and a simplistic solution to circumstantial difficulties*" (Bacca 1991, 13). A simple way to say this is that a corazonada is a sudden feeling regarding the correct approach to a certain problem (the "simplistic solution").

Returning to Uranga, and mirroring Bacca's definition, an "ontological corazonada" is *a sudden heartfelt confidence that our being is thus and so*. Because reason, or rationality, does not give us this confidence or even help us articulate the "thus and so," a corazonada resembles a "following one's heart," recalling Blaise Pascal's notion of the heart as having its own reasons (Pascal 2003).[3]

A corazonada is thus much more than a hunch, courage, or a gut feeling—it is a recognition carried out by the heart, which grants us "heartfelt certainties." Uranga uses the example of the poet, pointing out that the poet's access to being is not one of foreboding or presentiments, or *anticipations*, but is broader and more encompassing of existence as such. Thinking of it as an instrument of the poet, a "corazonada" is an immediate affective interaction with the poet's "lived experience" in all of its richness. Upon *reading* the interaction, non-poets in turn interact with that experience itself in its "pure" form in acts of immediate "translation." Through such interactions, I thus experience the world without the limitations imposed by perception or reason but with my heart, in feelings, affectively, rather than through a previously fabricated, totalizing, and exclusionary, rationality.

I thus propose the following definition of "corazonadas ontológicas" (following Uranga and Baccca): an *affective source of ontological truth grounded on non-mediated encounters with (or an pre-theoretical immersion in) our own, situated and determinate, circumstance.* Or, an ontological corazonada is that non-rational confidence that something is the case as justified immediately via my connection to the context in which I find myself.

As with most concepts derived from Mexican philosophy, corazonadas ontológicas will have a context, which is the emotional environment in which one lives and that informs us, a context that is ultimately familiar and that frames and nourishes our emotional understanding of the world, allowing us to *encounter* the world with confidence and certainty (much like Don Quixote). In what follows, I propose that we can apply this concept broadly to epistemological cases as well—if we remove the "ontological" from "corazonada" or "intimation"—those where knowledge cannot be adjudicated by either intuitive givenness or conceptual analysis.

This emphasis on its affective dimension or its immediacy does not mean that corazonadas, ontological or otherwise, are non-conceptual or non-discursive. Because a corazonada is a source of *truth*, it cannot be entirely outside the space of reasons. They seem to involve a level of cognition and rationality necessary to understand the world *as* familiar or as *my world*.

The goal in what remains is to clarify the nature of corazonada, ontological or otherwise (Section 1), which requires us to highlight its difference from intuition, a concept that Uranga considers limited and "confusing" (Section 2). I will thus briefly go over the idea of intuition as inherited from Kant and Husserl and highlight its variation in Bergson and Heidegger (a difference that supports Uranga's judgment about its confusing nature). Interestingly, the concept of "gut feelings" (which some consider the proper translation of "corazonadas") has recently entered the fray as an epistemological candidate of sorts, so I will briefly consider the nature of gut feelings (Section 3). I will end by highlighting the manner in which attending to *corazonadas ontologicas* can enrich our understanding of ourselves and our world.

1. Corazonadas ontológicas/Ontological Intimations

In his *Analysis of Mexican Being*, Uranga finds that the object of his study, namely, Mexican *being*, requires multiple access points. These include history, poetry, philosophy, and Mexican life itself. The last of these can be accessed in various ways, one of which is the corazonada. Uranga proposes that one can have a corazonada (an intimation) of certain particularities of Mexican life that the other points of access can't give. The corazonadas will be immediate, recognizable, and justificatory of claims regarding what it means to be Mexican—even if how they do this is not entirely rational.

Proposing corazonada as an entryway into the meaning of being, Uranga (2021) emphasizes that he seeks an alternative, not to history or poetry or, even, reason, but to "the confusing concept" of intuition (101). Intuition is confusing because it will have different abilities and powers depending on who one asks. Husserl, for instance, proposes that intuition is the *only* source of truth and justification, while Heidegger thinks of it as a derivative form of understanding that doesn't actually grant us any sort of privileged access. (I'll return to the "confusing" nature of intuition in the following sections).

Ultimately, intuition is not capable of securing the sort of evidence required to speak of something like *Mexican being*. What we need is a less restricted, more encompassing instrument and this is the corazonada ontológica. He tells us what he means in the following passage:

> *There are analyses that do not appear ontological, but that when looked at more closely show themselves almost immediately as direct "translations" of lived experiences . . . "'corazonadas' ontológicas."* This is the case with poetry. Being speaks through the poet in its own language. Poetry does not translate the being of its experiences into terms alien to being itself, but it comes to the reader in an almost pure form. This is why the ontology of the Mexican has to lend attention to the work of our poets with a degree of attention that will never be sufficient. Poetry has spoken more than the historians, psychologists, or sociologists about the being of the Mexican.
>
> In this way, the contributions of the poets will be of immense value to the analysis of the being of the Mexican—analyses such as those we find in Octavio Paz's *The Labyrinth of Solitude*. The poet lives in a most intimate familiarity with being; he has being ready to hand, so to speak. It is clear that we cannot give a formula that will teach us with mathematical regularity in which way the philosopher will translate what the poet says into properly ontological terms. It is a work of instinct and thought—two things, that is, that allow us to save ourselves from the confusing concept of intuition—and of flexibility and rigor. (Uranga 2021, 100/101).

I quote here at length because in this passage we find the main characteristics of *corazonadas*. They are:

(i). "direct,"
(ii). "immediate," and
(iii). "translations" of lived experience.

Moreover, their translatability and immediacy require

(iv). "intimate familiarity," involve
(v). a mixture of "instinct and thought," and require
(vi). "flexibility and rigor."

If we imagine the corazonada that motivates Don Quixote's passionate pursuit of his love-ideal, we find that it is a *direct, immediate, translation* of the world in which he exists, in which he *is*, one with which he is "intimately familiar," where chivalry, bravery, and sacrifice matter, and where love can be won by these. Because of those intimate ties with his world, the corazonada cannot be blind but will share in the space of reasons that structure that world, and in this way, as Uranga puts it, it will be a mixture of "instinct and thought." The corazonada, on this account, will be an active translation of the instinct, or a *spontaneous* and "instinctual" interpretation of that which makes sense relative to that with which one is intimately familiar. This mediated immediacy refers both to an affective, noncognitive familiarity that grounds our *heartfelt certainty* that something is the case and the sense-making cognitive capacities that allow this certainty to play a role in our thinking and behavior.

This allows us to see the value of corazonadas for the investigation into what it means to be Mexican. In *Analysis*, Uranga commits himself to the phenomenological demand to allow this being to speak for itself. However, because being will always overflow our human abilities to conceptually grasp it (this is the idea that being will overflow the concept), Uranga must expand the field of what can be given to cognition to include that which is not necessarily seen, what we may know by virtue of simply being around it, living through it, or interacting with it.

Corazonadas appear as that which give us access to that which overflows our rational conceptualizations, and it gives us this access in ways that may seem overly sentimental, and even accidental.

Before arriving at [the context in which *we know* about Mexican existence], we are completely at a loss, and *it seems that if we have gotten close to a shadow or region of the appropriate horizon [of that being], we have done so only by "corazonada."* And now we are in the right context from which the "things themselves" can speak. (Uranga 2021, 119; italics are mine)

What this means is that knowledge of being itself, when in its particularity (e.g., its Mexican particularity), may be arrived at *un-intentionally*, without rational awareness, and "only" by an immediate affective encounter that does not obey the laws of intuition, as, for instance, Edmund Husserl would require (see later). As we will see, the process is more of an interfacing and a bodily involvement in the sense of intuition described by Henri Bergson (see later discussion).

In my own case, as a Mexican American, a corazonada delivers me to the reality of my own nepantla before any and all conceptual articulations are made. This corazonada is given within the "horizon," or circumstance, which is my "proper context" and from which my nepantla-being "speaks" on its own, without my rational probing or desiring. As a mixture of reason and instinct, the corazonada is not an impersonal or "cold-blooded" measure of what there is but is sympathetic and open to what may offer itself and overwhelm it. This tracks Uranga's (2021) description:

For López Velarde, the definition of a new being of the Mexican must be achieved not so much "in cold blood," but through a "corazonada". More precisely, more than merely arriving at that being, that being must surprise us, violently and suddenly [*a manera de rapto*], in such a way that it solicits and takes possession of our thinking. "The alchemy of the Mexican character does not recognize any instrument capable of identifying its components of grace and solemnity, heroism and apathy, carelessness and cleanliness." . . . Can we now say that we have at our disposal an "instrument" capable of specifying the elements that make up our being? (165)

Grace, solemnity, heroism, apathy, carelessness, cleanliness—these, like nepanlta, lo mexicano, Chicano ambition, and so on, cannot be captured by our inherited, Western, philosophical instrumentality. Intuition or logical analysis operate "in cold blood," and are thus insufficiently suited to capture genuine human elements of experience: that which cannot be seen, but felt, such as grace; that which escapes logical analysis but can still affect community, such as apathy; that which can come from nowhere, and define a generation, such as heroism; and so on. A corazonada, on the other hand, allows us access even to those aspects of experience that may "surprise us, violently and suddenly," and possess us as they do, that may "take possession of our thinking," such as the delicate aura of grace and love, the sentimental force of nepantla, or the nuanced mechanics of ambition.

The upside of elevating the epistemic privilege of corazonadas ontológicas/ontological intimations is that the world itself grows larger and richer. Not confined to the horizon of cognitive graspings, the space of justification expands to include the emotional habitat in which I live, namely, my familiar circumstance, as well as the non-conceptual, mysterious, profound, and absolutely other elements of my everyday experience. My very being is exposed; being itself gives itself on its own accord, surprising and possessing me.

All of this points to a new, or other, philosophical methodology, one equipped with a different sort of instrument. What cannot be seen is *intimated*, even if in echoes and traces. This is all justificatory; this is all formative and influencing of behavior and identity. Uranga calls his corazonada-influenced methodology "auscultation," a term that in other contexts refers to the act of carefully listening to the human body so as to reveal its internal processes. In Uranga's analytic, auscultation is the method whereby the depths of Mexican being are explored with the heart, which listens and waits for them to speak. We find this methodological committment in Henri Bergson (1912) as well (as follows), which he describes as a method which gets "as near as possible to the original itself as possible, to search deeply into its life, and so, by a kind of *intellectual auscultation*, to feel the throbbing of its soul" (36). For his part, Uranga (2021) writes:

> our character, that structure of our being that history has bestowed upon us, has been "executed" from the impressive depths of ontological auscultation. It has been revealed to us as permanently fatalistic, in a dangerous communication with limit situations, and from this unending dialogue with the physiological and foundational aspects of human being, there has emerged a mode of being on which find an original layer of being that has been informed by everything. (122)

An ontological corazonada compliments an ontological ausculation in the same way that a shovel compliments a dig. The project here is finding the truth of being, and the tools are those analytic strategies required to find it—corazonada is one such tool.

To summarize, a corazonada ontológica is a product of the immediate, affective, coincidence between self and being. To experience our reality through it is to experience a reality that, while revealing something new, is *already familiar* and *already given* in previous intimate, nontheoretical, encounters. The corazonada offers heartfelt certainty because the purity of the experience has not yet been filtered by rational analysis. A corazonada is, in this way, an experience of certainty rooted in the immediacy of an affective encounter with a familiar state of affairs. With this, we mean that corazonadas ontológicas are rooted in the emotional context in which we live and which informs us, one that is familiar and which nourishes our sympathetic understanding of the world. Thus, they allow us to *encounter* the world otherwise than in an intuition.

Needless to say, the promotion of corazonadas to a level of epistemic privilege is not meant to eliminate or replace the value of rational analysis. Some truths of Mexican existence are buried deep in the Mexican soul, in its history, and in the working of culture, and will be grasped by reason, through the persistent efforts of critique and autognosis. However, a complete hold of this being is only possible (as far as such a "complete hold" of truths can be possible at all) by opening one's heart and allowing that being to surprise us, to show itself on its own terms, in an encounter in an intimate heartfelt encounter.

2. The Confusing Concept of Intuition

2.1 Kant and Husserl

Uranga appeals to corazonadas ontológicas because, he claims, the concept of intuition is "confusing" (Uranga 2021, 101). By this, he means that its definition and its capacities change from one philosopher to another, from one philosophical system to another, and even within one system and one philosopher. Thus, intuition means one thing in Max Scheler and another in Edmund Husserl, and then it means different things in Husserl, where we find, for instance, categorical and perceptual intuition, intuition of essences, and empirical intuition. More than being confused, however, intuition is also limiting; it is limited to the realm of presence or presencing.

Keeping to our nepantla example, we get a sense of the trouble with intuition if we ask: can *my* nepantla be given in an intuition? Again, it depends on how intuition is understood. Is it a sort of pre-theoretical, precognitive, knowing ("My intuition is that I'm neither Mexican or American but something in between") or is it a kind of perceptual experience that serves as a source of justification ("I have an intuition of my nepantla on speaking Spanglish"). With intuition in the first sense, *I feel strongly* that, in terms of my identity, I am neither Mexican nor American, but am suspended somewhere in the middle. However, the lack of cognitive content with this type of intuition makes it epistemically suspect. With intuition in the second sense, however, an intuition that would adequately fulfill the concept of nepantla, of a being in between, would require a kind of presence that the phenomena itself makes impossible.

Consider Immanuel Kant's notion of intuition. For Kant, intuitions are of two sorts, "empirical" or "pure"; the latter are those that supply content to the understanding, that fulfill concepts so that they may count as knowledge; the former are those that have no "mingling of sensation" (Kant 1999, A50/B74) and "contain the form" that makes possible sensible intuitions (space and time are "pure" intuitions). On this account, if nepantla were to be adequately given in intuition, it would be given in an empirical intuition, since it is not a pure form that makes possible the experience of something else.

However, the empirical intuition of being nepantla is also impossible. In the Transcendental Aesthetic of his first *Critique*, Kant (1999) writes:

> In whatever way and through whatever means a cognition may related to objects, that through which it relates immediately to them, and at which all thought as a means is directed as an end, is intuition. This,

however, takes place only insofar as the object is given to us; but this in turn, is possible only if it affects the mind in a certain way. This capacity . . . to acquire representations . . . is called sensibility. Objects are therefore given to us by means of sensibility, and it alone affords us intuitions. (A 19/B 33)

With Kant, the presence of the object is required for knowledge; there needs to be something there that "affects the mind." As he famously puts it, "concepts without intuitions are empty, intuitions without concepts are blind" (Kant 1999, A51/B75). In this sense, the concept of nepantla, like God or the soul, is empty; its intuition, if any is possible, is missing.

The same is true for Edmund Husserl. Husserl (1983) codifies the centrality of intuition in his Principle of All Principles, which states: "every originary presentive intuition is a legitimizing source of cognition, that [is] everything originarily [. . .] offered to us in 'intuition' is to be accepted simply as what it is presented as being, but also only within the limits in which it is presented there" (44). Here, Husserl echoes Kant's assertion about empirical intuition, and further enshrines it as a justificatory source of knowledge. *Only* those things that are experienced can be given in intuition and only those things given in intuition are legitimizing sources of knowledge. Husserl thus bestows upon intuition full justificatory authority. Intuition is the true and only source of knowledge; intuition is experience itself: "for experience we therefore substitute something more universal: 'intuition'" (37).

In both accounts, Kant's and Husserl's, intuition (pure or sensible) is always at work within the realm of presentation or representation and does not stray far from there. Husserl (1983) writes: ". . . we allow *no* authority to curtail our right to accept all kinds of intuition as equally valuable legitimating source of cognition" (39). On the flip side, this means that intuition will not give us evidence that falls outside the sphere of presentative givenness. The exceptions are mathematical relations and the categories of space and time, which for both Husserl and Kant are given in different kinds of intuitions, namely, categorical and pure, respectively. However, while categorical and pure intuition grant us access to concepts and categories necessary for human understanding, they are not useful in picking out existential or ontological experiences related to our emotive being human. In short, if something falls outside the space of intuitive givenness, then it cannot inform what we think we know.

2.2 Bergson and Heidegger

Then again, intuition need not be limited by presence. Other conceptions of intuition allow it to see into those spheres closed off to presentative intuition. One such account is offered by Henri Bergson.

In his *Introduction to Metaphysics*, Bergson (1912) refers to "intuition" as a type of "intellectual sympathy" (69). This is already a radical departure from Husserl, for whom intuition represents a *direct* access to the given, and not simply a *sympathetic* and, thus, an indirect access. Bergson acknowledges that some presentations will not offer themselves in their totality, but reserve for themselves their mystery. For Bergson, then, "intuition" brings about "[i]ntuitive knowledge which installs itself in that which is moving and adopts the very life of things" (74). That is, intuition penetrates reality and finds what simple perception cannot. As such, it is much more than perception; it is an effort, he says, "to place ourselves directly at the heart of the subject, and to seek as deeply as possible an impulse, after which we need only let ourselves go" (90). Bergson writes: "For we do not obtain an intuition from reality—that is, an intellectual sympathy with the most intimate part of it—unless we have won its confidence by a long fellowship with its superficial manifestations" (91). This "long fellowship" or apprenticeship in reality suggests that the thing intuited is familiar, part of the circumstance and inscribed in the environment. Having "won its confidence," the world *opens itself* to our examination.

While Bergson's notion of "intellectual sympathy" suggest that intuition is still bounded to cognition, to reason, and thus to justificatory presence, he imbues it with the capacity to *feel* itself into what presents itself so as to access that aspect of the experience that is not given. This sort of sympathy compliments rational cognition; this sort of sympathy completes knowledge. Thus, he writes, "we have the feeling of a certain very determine tension" when we encounter the object (Bergson 1912, 58), a tension that is certainly not an object of and for intuition as authorized by Husserl's Principle of All Principles, but necessary to understand the object fully.

Nevertheless, although intellectual sympathy grants us access to what is not seen, that is, the inner workings of the given, it nonetheless appears as a fully cognitive act and thus bounded by presence. In other words, something needs to be seen in order for intellectual sympathy to operate. Bergson (1912) says:

> it is impossible, even with an infinite number of accurate sketches, and even with the word "Paris" which indicates that they must be combined together, to get back to an intuition that one has never had, and to give oneself an impression of what Paris is like if one has never seen it. (28)

Bergson's notion of intuition is expansive, but there must be an original seeing to which one can return, a ground of perception that makes possible a more profound probing. He calls this profound probing "intellectual auscultation":

> a true empiricism is that which proposes to get as near to the original itself as possible, to search deeply into its life, and so, by a kind of *intellectual auscultation*, to feel the throbbing of its soul; and this true empiricism is the true metaphysics (36).

Uranga talks about "auscultation," but this is "ontological" and not "intellectual." The difference rests on the sort of "instrument" used: in Uranga, that instrument is emotive, in Bergson, it is intellectual, which takes us back to the limits of cognition and the confusing nature of intuition. The focus on intellect implies the need for a cognitive grasp which is but a part of a greater, more encompassing, grasping possible in more emotive, and embodied, experiences.

From a distance, intuition as intellectual sympathy is similar to Uranga's corazondas ontológicas: they both access that which is mysterious about the world in ways that involve both affect and intellect.

The difference lies in that for Bergson the actualization of intellectual sympathy is tied to perception as ground and is one-directional—the object is there to be examined and probed, itself surrendered to the auscultation; for Uranga, on the other hand, corazonadas are free of that tie to perception and the object and the subject come together in an immediacy and familiarity which is not intentional but affective and embodied. The auscultation, that is, involves more than the mind—it involves also the heart.

And finally, Heidegger. With Heidegger, intuition loses its epistemic privilege. In Heidegger's existential phenomenology, consciousness and understanding, and thus intuitions, are recast as derivative, all taking a backseat to doing and being. This means that intuitions are not *immediate* encounters with the world, as Husserl and Kant claimed, since this kind of immediacy is not available as a phenomenological observable. Heidegger (1962) puts the matter to rest rather abruptly when he writes:

> By showing how all sight is grounded primarily in understanding . . . we have deprived pure intuition of its priority, which corresponds noetically to the priority of the occurrent in traditional ontology. "Intuition" and "thinking" are both derivatives of understanding, and already rather remote ones. Even the phenomenological "intuition of essences" is grounded on existential understanding." (187)

Here, Heidegger also places the burden of *knowing the world* on understanding, which is an existential category and not cognitive instrument. This is another way to say that being is primary, knowing secondary.

Much could be said about Heidegger's dismantling of traditional metaphysics, but this brief comment on intuition will suffice to show the "confusing" nature of the concept and the reason why Uranga thought it best to appeal to "corazonadas ontológicas." Ultimately, corazonadas are not intuitions in the Kantian or Husserlian sense. They are, if intuitions are the measure, closer to what Bergson means by the term. A more accurate comparison can be made with Blaise Pascal's notion of the heart, as a site of reasons—this idea preserves the place of the "corazón," or heart, so it makes sense. According to Pascal, there are justificatory reasons that are not cognitive, but affective, and which are rooted in the feeling of heartfelt certainty. Pascal's oft-quoted truism that "the heart has its reasons that reason does not know" is the most obvious bridge between "corazonada" and the Western philosophical tradition (Pascal 2003, 78). Even if we do not take Pascal's dictum literally, and say that by "heart" (or, *corazón*) he means something else, like a "feeling" or a "passion," the relevant epistemological mechanism remains: a noncognitive affective confrontation with *something*. For Pascal, the "heart" is the emotive, spiritual, access to that which reason cannot grasp, with what stands outside its limits, or, even, overflows them: God and the divine, the revelations of scripture, holiness, and so on.[4] Similarly, we can say that a "corazonada" is that affective encounter with a non-conceptual reality that is *known* outside the space of articulated reasons, namely, a Mexican reality that is known (in this immediate, noncognitive way) to Mexicans who live it and experience it.

Finally, a corazonada ontológica challenges the privilege of intuition by revealing itself as a different sort of "instrument." It is *other* to intuition in a very real way; as an epistemological entryway into the mysteries of being, it does not obey the logic of epistemic validity required by the principle of adequation (*adaequatio rei et intellectus*). In fact, as has been hinted, the corazonada is an almost accidental, heartfelt certainty, unrestricted by the concept's ability to regulate what will fulfill it.

3. Gut Feelings

In trying to figure out a proper translation for corazonadas, I asked native Spanish speakers about how they would translate it. A common answer was, "gut feelings." On the face of it, this seems like a false equivalency. Corazonadas are, at least metaphorically, rooted in the heart; gut feelings are, at least metphorically, rooted in the stomach or gut. On this very superficial reading, the former is thought to grant us an emotively filled access to the world; the latter a physiological one. This difference lies in that I can be emotional about something without physiologically reacting to it (e.g., the nostalgia for my lost love), and I can physiologically react to something without feeling emotional about it (e.g., when onions trigger my gag reflex). However, emotions are embodied, and so gut feelings can be tied to the way in which my entire embodied being reacts to what it knows with certainty and will do so immediately. So where does the difference lie between corazonadas and gut feelings?

In contemporary scholarship, Ditte Munch-Jurisic appeals to neurophysiological research, the phenomenology of emotions, and various kinds of testimony to arrive at a theory of gut feelings that brings this concept closer to Uranga's notion of "corazonada." The overall idea is that gut feelings are bodily reactions to external stimuli that contain in themselves a degree of cognitive certainty resembling knowldege and upon which we act in one way or another. Munch-Jurisic (2018) reflects on the nature of "perpetrator disgust," or the disgust felt by the perpetrator of a gruesome or morally ambivalent act. Disgust is thought as an emotion which is "an embodied form of moral resistance and, as such, an important source of moral judgment and potential moral action" (142). In being disgusted, the perpetrator, in this sense, somehow *knows* that his act is immoral, although he cannot articulate it; the perpetrator who feels disgust is said to have a "gut feeling" that what he is doing is wrong, which for this subject is a source of knowledge that may either embolden him or dissuade from perpetrating his morally repulsive actions.[5]

The common notion of gut feelings conceives them as immediate *reactions* to external events, or as "instinctual," and as a primitive element of human nature. As such, they are thought in relation to other emotions like disgust and distress, which means that they are incapable of grounding the sort of *knowing* to which Uranga alludes. However, for Munch-Jurisic there is a cognitive element to gut feelings since one must be able to recognize what it is that provokes the *gut reaction*. Thus, gut feelings can contribute to knowledge and understanding in the sense that one can withdraw from what stimulates the feeling, reflect, and return to it in action—they can be sources of moral knowledge, as is the case with perpetrators. What this means, however, is that gut feelings (as other emotional reactions to external stimuli) are both rational and tied and conditioned to the environment or circumstance. Munch-Jurisic (2022) writes: "Emotions, gut feelings, and even rudimentary affect are not mere instinctive reflexes. They are inherently social, moral and political in a two-fold sense: They are both the product of our social, moral and political upbringing, and they continuously shape the way we act and think as social, moral and political beings" (6). The way this happens is, of course, complicated but rests on one key assumption: the agent is shaped and formed/informed by the circumstances in which she finds herself.

Munch-Jurisic refers to her view of gut feelings as "contextual." Because gut feelings are both cognitive (the internal context) and noncognitive (the external context), they involve judgment as well as instinctive physiological reactions, which are informed by the context, "allowing for the intricate and inseparable relationship between our affective states and the thoughts that accompany them" (Munch-Jurisic 2020b, 149).

> We even adapt and conform to norms that we may disagree with in principle, and we may not even notice the influence certain ideologies have on our behavior. In short, we internalize norms in the same way that we inhale the air around us. In a substantial sense, then, gut feelings are not simply private and individual, but public in source and constitution, part of a shared atmosphere. Gut feelings are shaped by the social and moral environment of the society and subcultures we belong to (Munch-Jurisic 2020b, 152).

Ultimately, gut feelings are a type of knowing that informs moral judgments, especially judgments with immediate moral implications.

We can conclude from this brief excursion into a phenomenology of emotions that corazonadas are gut feelings if understood in Munch-

Jurisic's contextualized sense, otherwise they are not. That is, they are not gut feelings if by that we mean a purely physiological reaction to what confronts me (which is the common usage). On the other hand, the immediately heartfelt recognition, or my corazonada ontolólogica, of my *nepantla* is both cognitive and noncognitive, an instinctive knowing couched in place and context and a conceptual grasping of a lived experience with which I'm very familiar.

4. Gut Feelings and Corazondas

However, we don't normally think about gut feelings in the contextualized way in which Munch-Jurisic describes them, namely, as contextualized physiological reactions. We think of them rather as fully physical reactions, located in or around the stomach, involving what scientists describe as "brain to gut signaling," a process that simultaneously affects our attitudes or moods (Mayer 2011).[6] If I have a gut feeling that my son is lying to me about his online activities, I am gradually overcome by the thought of his lying *to me* and I feel a "knot" in my stomach that *tells me* I am probably right—anger follows. Certainly, there is a context there: he's my son, I know him, I am also familiar with the possible online misadventures he may be involved in, he's also a teenager, and so on, thus, it is contextual in this sense. There is also a rational element involved, but that is more of a suspicion that remains until I do something to prove or disprove it. If I am *right* about my suspicion, then I say, "I felt it in my gut!" However, if, after looking for proof, it turns out that my suspicion is unfounded—say, he's actually crafting an outline for a fantasy novel—then, in this case, I say something like "my suspicion was wrong." My gut feeling is reduced to a suspicion subject to verification which is either fully physiological *when it is proved to be right* or fully rational (as a suspicion) *when it is proved to be wrong.*

Ultimately, I don't *know* if my son is actually lying to me. My gut feeling does not give me the knowledge I would need to know this to be true.[7] The case is different with corazonadas ontológicas of my Mexicanness or my nepantla. In those cases, I have heartfelt certainty that I am neither Mexican nor American, but suspended between both. There is usually no accompanying physiological reaction to this insight; I have it, and I know it to be true and authentic; my physiological reaction, if any, is limited to a sense of comfort or confidence and is not localized to my gut; there is no "brain to gut" signaling that takes place, rather, it is a "world to heart" signaling. This happens generally with cases tied to *knowing my way of life*, in which my reaction is one of heartfelt certainty, confidence, and trust that what has just come to my attention (my Mexicanness, for instance) is true regardless of the presence of an accompanying physiological reaction or a perception of contrary evidentiary facts. I am in the truth of the fact, and the way I arrived here is not entirely intelligible.

5. Conclusion

This chapter has dealt with the notion of "corazonadas ontológicas," "intimations," or simply, "corazonadas." These grant access to the mysteries of situated existence (e.g., Mexican being, Chicanx being, nepantla, etc.); they are epistemic and ontological interactions that grant us access into the secrets of a particular form of life. The upside of appealing to corazonadas ontológicas as sources of knowing is that the *emotional habitat* or circumstance is as significant as the material habitat or circumstance, so that those *modes of being a Mexican* to which Mexican philosophers appealed when talking about relajo, nepantla, and so on, are given immediately to anyone who can invest, or inhabit, or dwell, in the Mexican circumstance very broadly construed. Their mediated immediacy refers both to an affective, noncognitive familiarity that grounds our *heartfelt certainty* that something is the case and the sense-making cognitive capacities that allow this certainty to play a role in our thinking and behavior. Again, Uranga calls his corazonada-influenced methodology "auscultation," a term referring to the act of attentively listening to the human body so as to "know" its internal processes. In Uranga's philosophy, auscultation is the method whereby the depths of Mexican being are explored with embodied concern, that is, *with one's heart*.

Ontological corazonadas can also be useful in mystical experiences. The feeling, or sense, of oneness described in such experiences is not uncommon: suddenly, and without preface, one finds oneself before a power greater than oneself, certain greater than one's finitude, and at peace with what there is or with what may come. One arrives at such a state not via an intellectual recognition of the facts (intuition), nor via a physiological reaction to what appears (gut feelings), but by simply opening oneself and allowing an otherness to enter; it is a movement of surrendering the ego that is both and neither cognitive and noncognitive, expected and unexpected, familiar and absolutely strange. The question is not whether or not the event has taken place, but rather how one *knows* that such an event has occurred. The answer is simple: one just knows and one knows it in one's heart. It is not a hunch or the perception of the miraculous that tells one that something unexplainable has happened. One knows this to be the case in heartfelt certainty via a corazonada.

Or, finally, consider our knowing that our culture is a white supremacist culture. Certainly, signs will be there: police brutality against black and brown bodies; political and symbolic violence against the LGBTQ community; nativist immigration policies; and so on. For the most part, however, white supremacy will be hidden from sight by a variety of ideological obfuscations or behind media spectacle. But even without the obvious signs, we still know it is there. We know, in our hearts, that our difference is monitored and controlled by systems of oppression designed for us. Sometimes these systems are revealed in George Floyd-style explosions of white privilege. But for the most part, we just know where we stand, or where we are expected to stand, and we know this via faculties that are not straightforwardly cognitive or noncognitive—we know via ontological corazanadas that reveal us inserted amid power relations designed to suppress our being and our heart.

In Uranga's philosophy, the introduction of the notion of "corazonadas ontológicas" is meant to offer an alternative to "intuition," which on its own, and given its various significations, is confusing. Whether or not corazonada is a viable alternative, it certainly expands the field of justificatory evidence to include the whole of one's situated experience. The clue for this expansion is that when talking about those things that really matter, intuitions are sometimes not enough; we revert to pantomime, so as to say, "*I just know.*" This "I just know" is grounded on a corazonada, a heartfelt certainty that our belief (or action) is justified in some way.

Uranga found himself in this predicament, trying to find proof of his Mexicanness (of *lo mexicano*), and found himself *in the truth of this* on reading López Velarde, on *listening* to the inner rumblings of his own heart which itself attended to things that spoke on their own accord. The heart hears what is inaudible; it hears ontological truths —it hears what is real. Intuition can only allow so much to be seen and heard. Corazonadas, especially the ontological kind, expose us to a much broader universe of possible experiences. In my own case, I am before the heartfelt recognition that I am still Mexican even if my Mexicanness is hidden underneath my Anglo-American education, my Spanglish, and my official government designation. Ultimately, the concept of corazonada is an interruption, a valuable and useful tool in a world where much is hidden beneath the stubborn solidity of intuitive evidence.

Tik

(*teek*)

Overview of the Concept: *Tik is an indigenous concept describing an organic sense of community or we-ness* (un grupo nostrico). *Tik refers to an inclusive, participatory, plurality that prioritizes the needs, wants, and stability of the whole without denying the value of the individual, although it does deny the* priority *given to the individual by, for instance, Western humanism. That is, in a tik-community, individuals will contribute—through non-ideological dialogical practices internal to the history, culture, and traditions of the community—to a common vision and act toward that vision in acts of love, generosity, and self-sacrifice.*

We tend to refer to groups of people that are somehow contiguous and somehow related as "communities." Thus, we talk in general terms about the "immigrant community," or more specifically, about the "Vietnamese community" or the "African American community." Growing up, I learned from television, my high school counselors, and the news media that I belonged to the "Mexican community," although I don't recall ever *feeling* as if I was *part* of any community—yes, all my friends were Mexican, or Mexican American, my parents spoke Spanish at home, their friends were Mexican, family friends came by often to make *birria* and drink too much, they all worked hard, demanding jobs in the agricultural fields, and the legal system seemed a bit schizophrenic toward everyone we knew (people were either aggressively pursued or negligently ignored), but I don't remember feeling *a part of* a "community." What I knew was that we simply existed together in the same situation, doing similar things, living a similar life. In high school I learned that "*my* Mexican community" was known to place a great emphasis on family, education, hard work, and *community* itself. It was true that my mother demanded I go to school because she believed that this would be the only way that my life would be better than theirs, it was also true that my father worked harder than anyone I knew or have known since, but our family was dysfunctional and poor, and the "community" had never intervened to fix the dysfunction or the poverty. The "Mexican community," I concluded, was simply an idea, one to which I belonged either by political decree or via historical and cultural relations—forces over which I had no control. However, even as an idea, it existed then as it exists now.

In the United States, metanarratives insist that the Mexican *sense* of community is particularly strong and particularly formative. For instance, existing metanarratives talk about the value placed on the family by the traditional Mexican community—in spite of my own lived experience to the contrary. This value is verifiable in anecdotes and empirical studies by social scientists and artists: for decades scholars have emphasized the "cohesiveness and togethernesss" of the Mexican family (Diaz-Guerrero 1975), a conception that extends to the Mexican community outside of Mexico, as illustrated by an emphasis on "familialism" as a "structural feature" of the Mexican American family (Alvirez and Bean 2001, 224); in addition, current educational research reinforces this view, revealing that Latinx students value family and community above all else (see, Clayton et al., 2019; Sy and Romero 2008).

Mexican philosophers tried to make sense of, and arrive at the conditions for the possibility of, the "Mexican community," especially during the post-Revolutionary period. During this period (1920–60), the Mexican political establishment sought to reintegrate the country under a common nationalist identity, one that would unite people under a common flag so as to bring about national unity. The philosophical search for the essence of Mexicanness (lo mexicano), an identity that would characterize all Mexicans, is a consequence of this search. To find the essence of the Mexican is to find that commonality that would unite a plurality under a common existential struggle.

However, finding that commonality does not guarantee community. The appropriate *sense* of community is hard to come by, and community itself is always under threat from rampant individualism, or, even, relajo. In Jorge Portilla's analysis of community, for example, individualism or relajo can easily instigate a process of social disruption or dis-unity whereby that which holds the community together no longer works (see Sánchez and Gallegos 2020).

So as to avoid an inevitable disintegration, Portilla reconsiders the phenomenon of community. He suggests a conception of community founded on an "us both." This is a phenomenological conception that seeks to distance itself from existing notions of community. Portilla's approach, however, suffers from not being radical enough. On Portilla's account, talking about a "Mexican community," or "Mexican American," "Vietnamese American," or "African American" community is reduced to mere (fragile) encounters between people.

Broadening the bandwidth of the "Mexican philosophical tradition," we include Mexican indigenous philosophies where we find other, more nuanced, complex, and novel conceptions of community—conceptions that are truly and radically non-Western. These radical non-Western conceptions of community are not threatened by the weight of individual self-interest and, in fact, offer an antidote to my fragile notion of community or that envisioned by Portilla. I am thinking here of indigenous philosophical traditions that are both "Mexican" in the political sense of being historically and socially bound up with Mexico as a nation, and in the philosophical sense of being reflections of the Mexican circumstance understood as a lived experience.[1]

It is in this context that we introduce the Tojolab'al[2] concept of "tik," which refers to the sort of cohesive, inclusive, and participatory community that could serve as an aspirational ideal for both Mexican philosophy and for ourselves.[3]

"Tik" is translated alternatively as "we," or "us," and it seeks to preserve the self in the accomplishment of a fully participatory community—*tik* is we-ness, and not I-ness, it is the primordial ontological ground, the essence of the self as inclusion and participation in community.

Simply put, community, we-ness, is *all-there-is* and is the very ground of being and thinking. Ultimately, I propose that tik is consistent with the philosophical project of a nepantla Mexican philosophy as outlined in the Introduction, a radical departure from the Western worry over individuality and subjectivity, and more importantly, a resource in the conceptual arsenal of Mexican philosophy as a more inclusive global philosophical tradition.

A brief incursion into Portilla's critique of community helps us set the stage for our discussion of "tik."

1. The Problem with Community: Jorge Portilla

Portilla gives us a critique of Western notions of community (Sections 1.1–1.2) and offers a phenomenologically inspired alternative (Section 1.2.4). His alternative, however, is insufficient due to its prioritizing of the individual as the ground for community. The Tojolab'al concept of "tik" avoids these issues and more.

1.1 The State of Sub-Integration

According to Portilla (2017), of the various crises diagnosed by Mexican philosophy mid-way through the twentieth century, the most pernicious is "the state of sub-integration" of Mexican society (189). Sub-integration is the state whereby individuals lose their sense of belonging and suffer from "a species of social malnutrition" (189) and no longer feel nourished by the social or communal relation.

As Portilla observes, "community in Mexico is lived at a distant and unarticulated horizon that does not offer a precise orientation or consistent support for individual action" (190). This happens when individuals no longer feel part of, or integrated in, something greater than themselves, coping with this loss of belonging in destructive and counter-productive ways (e.g., relajo). Sub-integrated individuals will ultimately seek their purpose in factions, sects, and parties that reflect the narrow ideological horizon of their own personality, becoming in this way "super-integrated" (e.g., apretados). Because it ultimately tends toward a denial of community as an inclusive relation and toward hyper-specialization and exclusion, super-integration is, Portilla says, "without a doubt . . . an evil" (189).

Super-integration feeds on sub-integration. An example would be the way in which militant extremism feeds on modern economic alienation. For Portilla, this condition of super-and sub-integration reflects the *dis*integration of community by an "extreme" and "bourgeois individualism" that halfway through the twentieth century, plagues all sectors of society and is responsible for the predominance of zozobra, fragility, resignation, and relajo. However, it is not blatant individualism itself that has weakened the Mexican sense of community; rather, its weakening has more to do with the fact that the sense of community has become "confused" or vague. Portilla goes on to propose a way to think of a community that is not vulnerable to the disengagement of the individual from his sense of community. This is a phenomenological, "relational," notion of community. As we will see, however, this sense of community is flawed, depending as it does on the power of the individual to maintain himself in a certain communal relation.

1.2 Existing Notions of Community

Portilla (2017) suggests that existing "sociological" notions "are not useful for us" because they are "overly general" and "universal" (180). He has in mind here "sociological" theories that define community as "a form of organic association . . . in which" one finds oneself "always already . . . developing within it . . . moved by spontaneous impulses, by a species of essential will" which is "non-accidental" and "untouched" by individual action (180). Ultimately, these notions are too abstract to account for the "concrete" and "specific structure of the Mexican community" as he lives it (181).

So as to arrive at his own position, which he calls community as an "us-both," Portilla discusses three conceptions of community:

community as person, community as horizon, and community as an "us."

1.2.1 Community as Person

To think of community as a person is to imagine it capable of answering for itself, acting on its own, or forging its own path. To it, one can attribute intentionality and purpose. On this conception, it is normal for us to say things like "Russia's aggressive rhetoric threatens international security" or "the Vietnamese community in San Francisco seeks more rights." In this example, both Russia and the Vietnamese community are thought about as persons or intentional entities. According to Portilla, however, this is a "vague concept of community" (181) that assumes a relational unity that does not exist.

The problem with such conceptions is that they invite external "objectifications" of the whole community without regard to the differences that may exist within it. The community is "one" intentional entity. Ultimately, this external conception of the community becomes the standard through which the community is judged; *real* interpersonal relations become secondary to the *image* of the overall community, its reputation, and the appearance of its unity; the end result is the fetishization of the community or its transformation into spectacle. Examples of this include the fetishization of indigenous communities all over the Americas for various reasons, some political others commercial, but all blind to the differences within or between those communities themselves.

1.2.2 Community as Interpretive Horizon

The second sense of community considered by Portilla is the sense of community as interpretive horizon, or "community as a horizon in which actions are articulated, or as the horizon for the comprehension of certain actions, and some would say for the majority of our human actions" (183). The community, that is, is held together by a shared interpretive horizon that serves as the backdrop against which our thoughts, actions, and beliefs make sense or fail to make sense; the community serves as a "wall against which the meaning of our actions bounces back like an echo" (184). As such, the community is an "interpretive community" where members share "strategies" and "assumptions" as they make sense of their world and their life in it (see Fish 1980).

The problem with this view of community, however, is that it seems like an artificial construction, one we can imagine surviving if the interpretive horizon were to collapse or disappear. Sure, one would be lost and confused in its absence, perhaps one would question one's sanity, but one would, apparently, persist. Portilla (2017) describes such a scenario:

> If suddenly a certain evil demon, playing a serious prank, were to conceal this horizon, we would suddenly find ourselves as if waking from a dream, incapable of understanding our very presence where we stand, incapable of understanding any of the actions taking place in it. The scene would seem to us very strange . . . we would walk away holding tightly to an incipient anxiety about the state of our mental faculties. (183)

Community as an interpretive horizon proves itself weak if only because of this possibility, namely, that it is vulnerable to disintegration— whether this vulnerability is due to evil demons or cultural paradigm shifts.

In reality, while the disintegration of a particular interpretive horizon is a possibility, our loss will be minimal because Portilla, like most contemporary philosophers, believes that we do not exist within just one such horizon, but many. We exist, Portilla proposes, in multiple communities at once, *intersected*[4] by multiple interpretive horizons, so that if one collapses, others remain:

> we also live in a multiplicity of communal horizons that mix and weave with one another and that always remain potential or actual, depending on whether our action reveals or conceals them. (183)

Now, the problem with this "multiplicity" view is that the sense of community is weakened when we think of community as splintered in this way. The weakness is due to the possible confusion created by the presence of multiple interpretive horizons simultaneously available to us, which could make it difficult to fully invest ourselves in one community. We would be, Portilla thinks, indecisively committed to multiple interpretive schemes that at times could overlap or at times contradict one another. "The result," warns Portilla, "is a weak political life . . . [because of] the bombastic ambiguity of the acts through which this life is manifested . . . [and] . . . a general not-knowing what to depend on . . ." (184).

Nevertheless, Portilla believes that Mexicans subscribe to the concept of community as horizon, which "suffers from a sort of failure or inarticulateness" that in turn explains why Mexicans "have lost their 'true north" (184). To lose one's "true north,'" in Portilla's diagnosis, means that one's interpretive horizons no longer offer the means to make sense of the world in a way that contributes to individual and communal flourishing. The Mexican community, because of this failure, cannot offer a backdrop of meaning capable of adjudicating parameters for the good life.

More seriously still, is that individuals chose not to subscribe to any communal horizon and, ultimately, set off on their own. What we end up with is a society where individuals make individual decisions that benefit only themselves, where each one is a "representative of his own personal interest," where we find, ultimately, "a failure of that sentiment of solidarity" (185) required by flourishing communities.

All of this points to a weakened sense of the concept of community, whereby the "communal horizon" appears "distant and unarticulated," constituting a reality that makes sub-integration possible and "serves as "the foundation of inactivity, of inaction, of that leaving-everything-for-tomorrow that is today a common trait of our character" (187). An unclear, or insufficient, conception of what community is supposed to be will only lead to uncertainty and vagueness about our own human projects. Alone, without a secure footing in our own community, we will find ourselves, individually, Portilla continues, "painfully exposed to the cosmic vastness" (189).

1.2.3 Community as "Us"

A third sense of community, one which, according to Portilla, is no better than the rest, is one where individuals believe themselves to be engaged in meaningful acts of world-making with one another and where self-interest is secondary to the transcendent interests of the "us." This is the sense of community as coexistence or as "us together." In this conception of community, "to exist is to co-exist" (190). "Us" is here a mediated relation; it is mediated by the idea of "us" *as a plurality tied together* by "a common transcendence" (190), that is, a common value that is greater than the sum of its parts and which is assumed in everything that we do. This "us," as a transcendent value, however, is inaccessible, remaining always as a mysterious remainder that nonetheless unites *us*. Community as this abstract "us" is problematic for this reason, namely, that the "us" is based purely on an "anonymous and blind contiguity" (192); a real, practical, relation is missing in the "us."

1.2.4 True Community: "Us both"

Portilla proposes that true community is only possible as an "us both" [*nosotros dos*]. Echoing the Buberian "I-Thou" relation (Buber 1986), Portilla argues that "us both" is a real, phenomenological relation where the actual presence of the "you" justifies the sense that "I" am *in* an authentic communal relation.

> True community is not given except in an "us" that is an "us both," a "you and I" for whom the relation is immediate, without the interposition of any previous scheme, without any conceptual game, or without an image. (Portilla 2017, 192)

While the "us" is merely an empty, formal, relation, the "us both" is an experienced relation, one given immediately to the both of us in an encounter. There is no horizon that justifies our relation as a you and an I, there is, moreover, no image to reflect, it is simply and immediately known that you and I are in communion and engaged in a similar project of existence. This is, Portilla says, a "living and authentic relation" (192).

Only this relation gives us the "interlacing of personal relations" which are the basis for authentic community. Because "a society without a face or warmth makes us cold with distrust" (Portilla 2017, 194), we must strive and work toward such an inter-active community; "our destiny as nation depends on our capacity to realize it" (195).

In the final analysis, Portilla appeals to the "us both" because other forms of community are either too abstract or too frail, relying on mystifications and superstitions that go beyond the realm of human experience. With the "us both," Portilla believes to be going between the horns of a hard individualism or a hard collectivism; he desires a middle ground, "where the Mexican finds his only communal dwelling" (194). The middle ground—nepantla—is the "authentic community" grounded on the "us both." He writes: "We can characterize the Mexican as a man who instinctively distrusts [collectivism and individualism] and who searches for an authentic community" (194).

2. Critique of Portilla

There are several problems with the identification of "us both" as authentic community. For one, "us both" points to nothing more than an encounter between two egos that can very well come undone if either abandons the relation. Also, everything depends on the encounter, which points to a community always already on the verge of disintegration since any encounter—as a temporal event—is always already ending.

Another problem with the "us both" is that it assumes that the encounter will always be between friends. Although this is not addressed by Portilla, it is possible that a community will be based on an "us both" which is antagonistic and violent. The one who confronts me with her face can be an enemy bent on my destruction.

Ultimately, my problem with this view is that it reaffirms the centrality of individuality, one where the individual takes priority over the community, as it is the individual's encounter on which everything depends, and if the individual encountered is violent or antagonistic, so will the community founded on the encounter.

The best alternative is the concept of the "us" that Portilla dismisses as compromised by abstractness. However, the "us" need not always be abstract, in which case, we ask, is it a better phenomenological description of community than the "us-both"?

To see how the "us" is not always abstract we look at the Tojolab'al notion of "tik," a reflection that should also help us broaden the horizon of "Mexican philosophy" while, simultaneously, further challenging the priority of the Western philosophical tradition.

3. The Tojolob'al Notion of Tik ("We"/"Us")

The German anthropologist Carlos Lenkersdorf (1926–2010) recounts the story of how he came to know and learn from the indigenous Tojolab'al people in southeastern Mexico (Lenkersdorf 2005).

Conducting ethnographic research in the Mayan region of Chiapas, Lenkersdorf was invited to attend a community gathering at a Tzeltal Mayan village. Neither he nor his team understood what was being said by those gathered, but they noticed a recurring vocalization, a *"tik"*-sound in every utterance.[5] Ignorant as to what this meant, Lenkersdorf and his team waited for the gathering to conclude and asked a local Jesuit priest regarding the meaning of "tik." The Jesuit informed them that it was a base concept specific to this region, present in both Tzetzal and Tojolab'al languages; it meant "nosotros," "we," or "us" (25). As the discussion was clearly related to matters critical to the community, "tik" was prominent in the discussion. Further inquiries revealed that "tik" expresses not only a linguistic trait specific to that region but also a central social and cultural motif. More significantly, however, it is learned that "tik" is the key to understanding the cosmovision of the Tojolab'al people.[6] For the next thirty years, Lenkersdorf lived and worked with the Tojolab'al, learning their language, their ways of life, and their philosophy.

Lenkersdorf's *Filosofía en clave tojolabal* or *Philosophy in the Key of Tojolab'al* (which serves as our primary source material and point of departure in what follows), seeks to tease out the philosophical significance of tik. In the process, Lenkersdorf introduces a concept that both compliments and goes beyond the Western conceptions of sociality or community, allowing us to think of the possibilities of and for the community in richer and more nuanced ways.

Tik is a key operative philosophical concept of the Tojolab'al— and, in fact, of Mexican philosophy when understood *broadly*. According to the Tojolab'al worldview, tik constitutes the conditions for the possibility of living and thinking. That is, one experiences and understands the world *through* a tik-perspective; or, plainly, we-ness is the primary hermeneutical framework. A philosophical interpretation of tik (in English "we" or "us," in French "nous," in Spanish "nosotros") will thus enrich our understanding both of this tradition and of philosophy itself.

In what follows, we consider the privilege of tik in this particular indigenous language, which, moreover, points to its centrality as an organizing social, epistemological, and moral principle for us all.

3.1 Tojolab'al Philosophy

The reason why Lenkersdorf pursues the meaning of tik is because he hears it over and over again. We could ask why repetition of this sort merits a philosophical analysis. In my own experience as an English-language learner, I had the same experience of linguistic repetition with the definite article "the" or the pronoun "I." One can imagine a more mature version of my ten-year-old self asking why "the" and "I" are so pervasive in the English language and what that pervasiveness means to the "cosmovision" of my Anglo-American classmates. This philosophically mature (and imaginary) ten-year-old would conclude, no doubt, that the speakers of this language truly value things (the field, the school, the teacher) and themselves (I, I am, I think, etc.). Of course, the ten-year-old me would not be too far off: speakers of this language do value the objects to which they refer and they truly value themselves (their individuality, their sovereignty, their autonomy, and so on).

Not surprisingly, Lenkersdorf does the same with tik and arrives at the predictable conclusion that the Tojolab'al value togetherness, community, sociality, we-ness, over and above either objects (*the* things) or their individual selves (I, myself). Of course, the concept of "tik" is more nuanced than being a mere placeholder or metaphor for community. Its place in the Tojolab'al cosmovision does more than represent the higher value placed on "us" versus "I." What tik, we-ness, or us-ness represents to the Tojolab'al is the very truth of being—everything is tik and everything means *though* tik; life, knowledge, and reality are grounded on and understood through tik as the central ontological principle. Lenkensdorf (2005) calls tik an "an organizing principle" (12), through which everything else is understood. In this, tik takes on the aspect of an interpretive horizon (of the "community as horizon," in Portilla's sense earlier). However, for the Tojolab'al the tik is not abstract, it is real, and there is never the danger of tik fragmenting or splintering into multiple horizons (or communities); it is the only framework, and that which is most real. Ultimately, the term itself is not problematized by the indigenous Tojolab'al as it is operative in all that they do and think.

Lenkersdorf's *Filosofía en clave tojolabal* is a first approximation of a somewhat systematic attempt to schematize an original indigenous philosophy in contemporary times. The title itself tells us that Lenkersdorf is prepared to rupture philosophy's hegemonic stranglehold on universality by saying that the philosophy here presented has a different voice, or is articulated in a different "key." If we stretch this metaphor, then, philosophy in general (or, more precisely, philosophy in a global sense) is a 2,500-year-old tune and the different philosophical voices (Eurocentric, Asian, African, Latin American, or Anglo-American) are but keys contributing to the notes and chords and movements of philosophy.

Tojolab'al philosophy could be called anti-colonial philosophy, as it is resistant to the maxims of Western philosophy. We can also call it postcolonial, as it is a philosophical worldview that has survived the colony and adapted, maintaining its difference in spite of coloniality. Truly, however, it is *simply philosophy*, as it seeks to capture a lived reality *as* this is experienced, revealing the transcendence of that experience, and thus enriching our understanding of the global human drama.

There is no word for "philosophy" in the Tojolab'al (or Tzetzal) language. The concept that captures the person who worries about the essence of thought and thinking is *"ayxa sk'u-jol,"* which means "he who has a heart" (Lenkersdorf 2005, 28). This concept captures a thinker who is *care-full* (full of care) with/about knowledge and also with/about others. As Lenkersdorf (2005) writes: "[Theirs] is a philosophy with heart, or better put, cordial, and not so intellectualized, but without rejecting thinking. It predominates, nonetheless, in humans 'with heart' and not among those with brains" (28). We could say that theirs is a philosophy grounded on *corazonadas*. Thus, to philosophize is to lend one's sensibility and empathy to the search for truth or the love of wisdom.

For us, "he who has heart," *"ayxa sk'u-jol,"* is a philosopher. And so when we refer to a Tojolab'al "philosophy" we include *care-fully articulated communal conceptions* of the world (those considerations rooted in empathy and care) that the original people would give about the nature and structure of their world. Such is tik.

Unlike the "us" that Portilla criticizes, the tik is real and its reality is manifested in the way that the Tojolab'al live in it and engage it: "The ubiquitous presence of the concept [of tik] characterizes not only philosophy in the key of Tojolab'al, but a philosophy that is well thought out, well reflected, and about which the Tojolab'al are very conscious" (12). Said differently, the Tojolab'al think about tik, they discuss it, and they organize their lives around it; moreover, they vary its possibilities and recognize its opposite, they know the anti-tik and they construct prescriptions against it; and, they affirm the reality of tik in both discourse and communal politics. Inevitably, Lenkersdorf points out, "[t]he *we . . .* becomes problematic [for the Tojolab'al], just as the I was so for Descartes, Freud, and other thinkers" (26).

3.2 Radical We-ness (Tik)

We find "tik" as a philosophical concept in contemporary indigenous philosophy, specifically, as a centerpiece in Tojolab'al philosophy, and include it as central to our broadly defined Mexican philosophical tradition.

"Tik" translates as "nosotros," which we translate as "we" or "us" (which will treat these as interchangeable). In ordinary, political, religious, or philosophical speech, the Tojolab'al speak and think from and through the perspective of a "we" or "us," an action that seems natural and immediate to the speakers. For the Tojolab'al, tik is *all-there-is*. As Lenkersdorf (2005) puts it: "the weight of this concept [tik] is extraordinary . . . it appears, disappears, and shines in places where it is least expected, from the social sphere to cyclical time, the numeric system and poetry" (12). This is to say that the concept tik grounds Tojolab'al beliefs, informing, in turn, their "figure of the world" (see Chapter 6), that is, their interpretive frameworks, and their language. As the Tojalob'al themselves say, "If you truly want to understand, to grasp our culture, and we say 'our culture' and not my culture nor his nor hers, but *ours*, truly *ours*, you will have to understand tik" (Lenkersdorf 2005, 34). Thus, we see it both as an originary interpretive horizon (epistemological aspect) as well as the actual, real, space of community (ontological aspect). Ontological, temporal, spatial, and other relations are organized via tik as that originary sense of togetherness—thus, *we* live time, *we* are number, and I exist only as an *us*. The "I," on this account, is only ideally an I, having reality only within this primordial organizing principle; the "us" is real or basic, the "I" abstract (contra Portilla's characterization of the "us" as the abstract term).

As real or basic, tik is a radicality that cannot be avoided. It is radical us-ness, and we-ness, a radicality "absorbs" the individual:

> Tik excludes the emphasis on the individual, on the particular ego. [It] absorbs the individual and demands his incorporation into the *we* [*tik*]—it demands the insertion of each one, man and woman, into the we-group [*grupo nosotrico*]." (13)

In other words, in the real relation which is "us" or "we," the individual does not exist, as it is folded *into* the relation itself. This "absorption" takes the form of an active, instinctive, and spontaneous participation in the aims and projects of the group. Tik "demands" this participation. Not behaving in accordance with the demand means not only that the individual thinks himself *more than* the group, but that he is *other* to the group; consequently, he is excluded from "we," a consequence that ironically, strips the individual of his individuality and identity, as without participation in tik he is no-thing and no-one. This means that exile into subjectivity or individuality familiar to the West is not possible in this worldview. For the Tojolab'al, any priority of the I is illusory, and there is no value to being an isolated "I," to being an ego, to being a self. There is thus no functional contrast between the we and the I. One is either in tik or one *is not*.

None of this means that there is no I. There is an I, but only within tik. Said differently, the self is not *lost* or erased or annulled in its "absorption" into an "us," rather, it is only within tik that the self can flourish and have a voice; but, again, not as a self, but only the community flourishes and speaks. That is, the consequence of the "absorption" into the we-group, or *grupo nosotrico*, means *not* a loss of self, but an affirmation of the self as an *us together*, as a together-people (a more populated version of Portilla's "us-both"). Lenkersdorf points out that this is the reason as to why it would be impossible to recognize a "famous" Tojolab'al thinker or philosopher, an *ayxa sk'u-jol*, for example. These do not exist in the public consciousness because there is no mechanism for this sort of individual to *identify* herself within tik.

Thus, the "we" ("us") supersedes and holds privilege over the "I" ("me") and the "you." It humanizes and lends reality to the I, to the subject, by being the horizon of its possibilities; its "internal structure is one that situates each of its members in a community context and demands their individual contribution" (Lenkensdorf 2005, 40). While the other may "complete" the subject (as in marriage), the I and you together must be embedded in the "we"; its structure is horizontal, and this demands that all members of the group assert themselves individually as members, without privileging their individual egos. In general, tik is ontologically and morally prior to the I and others by being the site of care and community.

In tik, each member is absorbed by the we-structure and in that space his or her uniqueness, his or her point of view blurs into a social project; the we-centric nature of tik synthesizes and subsumes all individual intentionalities into its own telos. This structure allows each member to make him or herself known, but only through what she or he contributes and not through a flash of personality, individuality, or unique perspective. In other words, tik "does not exclude the individual nor despise it, or annul it, but rather challenges it and waits for the best thought out contribution from each of its members" (Lenkensdorf 2005, 62).

This is the radical we-ness of tik. It involves more than the personal conscious states of individual subjects. It reconfigures the priority of "I think" as a "we think." We are no longer guaranteeing individual existence through an "I think," but, rather, vindicating the presence of a cosmic community through a "we think." Certainly, the priority of the "I think" has been challenged by Western philosophers in the past, for instance, Martin Buber's I-Thou or Emmanuel Levinas' Other. However, in those accounts it is ultimately the I that benefits and is strengthened by those encounters and those challenges. For the Tojolab'al, as it is with other original peoples, these "encounters" between an I and Thou or Other are isolated encounters that cannot happen outside the context of community. In other words, the I-Thou relation can only be understood as an I-we relation that cannot be exhausted in dialogical encounters between I and other I's or different thous. As the Tojolab'al themselves put it: "We do not negate the I, we do not erase it but the very I and the Thou only exist thanks to the existence of the *we* that gives these opportunities for them to develop" (Lenkensdorf 2005, 34).

The tik of the Tojolab'al is structured as an intersubjective arrangement, but it is not just that. While tik is certainly intersubjective, intersubjectivity is not necessarily tik, for the simple reason that tik is much more than a collection of subjectivities interrelated in the bare fact of being next to one another. In tik, as Lenkensdorf (2005) puts it, "[t]he whole of the *we* is more than the sum of the individual parts because it is the synthesized consensus" (62). While the notion of intersubjectivity assumes a collective made up of individual subjects that retain their own particular center of intentionality, tik absorbs intentionalities into itself while defusing intentionality throughout an amplified horizontal, bidirectional, or concentric structure. Moreover, the notion of intersubjectivity (as an abstract configuration of subjects before one another) lacks the relations of care, morality, or responsibility essential to tik, where "we are all subjects that need one another and we complement each other among each other" (115).

In tik the world is seen as made up of subjects who can never become mere objects. The tik-relation precludes objectification of subjects because only in this relation does the world make sense. Objects cannot correct me, or hear me, or remind me of things. But if mountains, and trees, and children, and those around me correct me and hear me and set me straight, then these cannot be objects, but part of the community, subjects without whom I could not understand the world or justify my own experience. A particularity about the Tojolab'al language underlines this point: if I, the author of this book, were to tell another person something about the weather and a few days later I were to remind that person what I had said, I would probably state this as: "I told you it would rain." With the Tojolab'al, however, this same sentiment can only be expressed by adding the actual presence of the other: "I told you that it would rain, and you listened to me telling you about the rain" (114). In English and Spanish, the other is assumed; in Tojolab'al, the other is always explicitly acknowledged.

3.3 Tik Is Not of a Single Mind

Tik is social and ultimately ontological bond that ties all members of the community together in a primordial or originary participatory enactment. This is an obvious, we could say *a priori*, or taken-for-granted, permanence reflected in a we-intentionality that orients every member toward the common good, a good inscribed in the very fabric of togetherness. This does not mean that all members of the community think exactly the same, nor is free-thinking actively discouraged, but this shared we-intentionality delimits a horizon of thought and action on which the Tojolab'al dwell as thinking subjects. It is this tik-relation, Lenkersdorf (2005) writes, that "orients everyone toward an agreement, rather than everyone speaking for themselves, convinced in his own ideas and pulling the rest in his own direction" (31).

Again, to exist in this radical we-ness does not mean that everyone thinks alike; the tik-orientation is inviting, argumentative, porous, heterogenous, and open. It does not close itself off to disagreement but allows it for the sake of flourishing and growth. This is because tik refers to a sociality that is constantly verifying its perspectives internally and externally, allowing doubt, communication, and agreement (or disagreement). Each of its members is expected to participate in this ongoing internal dialogue for the sake of the "we" that also communicates with others in global projects of solidarity. Accordingly, "tik does not correspond to the I that encloses itself in itself, that isolates itself from everything else, so as to obtain a firm and indubitable security of something that exists and that, precisely, it the thinking I" (31). This means that tik or us-ness is not paralyzed by its own private ideologies, activities, or worldviews, but precisely because it is porous and open, it keeps developing and expanding its borders and its reach—this is different, then, from the abstract and, ultimately, cultish "us" Portilla condemns earlier.

We can put the matter in the following way: the we-intentionality that describes the manner in which the Tojolab'al approach the world does not mean that the Tojolab'al are of *one mind*. Unlike the fictional *Star Trek* "Borg" who think as One, as a "Collective Mind," in accordance with a hive mentality, the Tojolab'al allow for individual opinions and divergence of thought. Each member is valued, not for their uniqueness but for what they, as persons, contribute to the group. There is self-awareness, but it is of the kind where "each individuality knows itself as incorporated in a we-ness that, consequently, is not the sum of individualities or parts, but rather represents a qualitatively distinct entity" (Lenkensdorf 2005, 32). We can say that for the Tojolab'al, tik is a *plurality of minds*, one that is not the collection of each mind reduced or synthesized into one, but a plural mind that retains each individual contribution gathered and oriented toward a common good. That is, tik is truly an *e pluribus unum* where the *pluribus* knows itself, always and explicitly, as having a place in, and existing because of, the *unum*.

Because tik is not of a single mind, because it preserves the integrity of individuals in dialogue, it does not demand the sort of justification for its own existence that plagues the self in the Western tradition. As Lenkersdorf put it: "Obviously . . . the experience of the *we* does not bring about the same Cartesian doubt nor does it direct itself toward the I, since this one is firmly integrated in the *we* that there is no need to mention it or question it" (31). Thus, "[i]t is, then, not the firmness or security of knowledge that disturbs the Tzotzil people, but rather the place of each speaker in the *us*" (31–2).

The sort of community that we are here discussing is rare. The self is not lost or negated in the Tojolob'al *tik*; what is negated is the self's privilege, its sovereignty, over and above others and the whole. There is no implicit imperative to be *self-less* or to lose the self, rather, the explicit imperative is to always do and say "in the name of the *we*" (32). That is, the imperative is to live radically with others. "The interest in oneself as an individual does not manifest itself nor is affirmed because each individual is what she is in so far as she is a member of the organism" (32).

3.4 Tik Is a Non-Ideal We

As Portilla rightly points out, Western philosophy has *idealized* the us-relation, which is why he thinks it is an abstract concept. From Plato to Kant the fully participatory community is placed as an ideal. The communal relation described by these thinkers is placed as an aspirational goal; this is the case with Plato's harmonious Republic (2007) or Kant's Kingdom of Ends (2012). These idealisms, however, lack an important property: they do not exist. Tik, on the other hand, is not only the very ontological ground of the Tojolob'al, but it is a *real* existing relation:

> The "we" is an unknown reality with a cosmic profile that, unexpectedly, reduces the importance that we like to assign to each one of us. The *we*, in so far as it is a total organism, establishes internal and external relationships that common thought cannot imagine. (Lenkersdorf 2005, 34)

In this way, tik functions as a leveling of egos and personalities. It has a *real* function, which is a function employed in the activity of community unfolding. In a certain sense, it *impersonally* organizes the various personal relations that make it up, while simultaneously assigning a role and identity to things. It is thus an ontological ground, one capable of structuring group and individual identity and the very nature of things *as understood* by the Tojolab'al.

As the non-ideal relational ground, expulsion from tik poses serious, existential, consequences. Individuals expelled from tik are ineffective as human beings—they have no role or function in human affairs. This is because, again, individuality itself rests on tik. As Lenkersdorf puts it, "[s]eparation from the rest . . . brings about the withering and loss of the individual" (32). In other words, individuality itself depends on *being-in* tik. If one finds oneself outside the tik-structure, one "withers" away. But even *in* the tik-relation, one must be *with* others; one cannot, that is, isolate when in the community. Consider the example of being a bachelor. In Tojolab'al culture, "single people are not considered complete" (Lenkensdorf 2005, 39). To be an unmarried man is to exist as an incomplete *individual*. This speaks to the sense of being a human person only in relation to others; an incomplete person is not a full person. Marriage completes the person because it ties that person to another in a tik-relation; however, this is not enough since the complete (married) person's life is meaningless if it is not tied to the larger community. In the Tojolab'al cosmovision, alienation, isolation, or solitude degrades human existence itself to its lowest degree: being with others is the highest form of existence, followed by being with another, and finally, and least important, being with oneself.

This is all to say that tik is not merely an ideal, but the most real and the *all-there-is*, a reality that is seen and lived by the Tojolab'al as an everyday fact. A final example of *tik's* reality: Lenkersdorf (59–61) recounts the experience of teaching Spanish at the Tojolab'al village. To Lenkersdorf's surprise, at one point in the course the students asked to be tested on what they had learned. It was surprising because the idea of "examinations" was foreign to the Tojolab'al, but they insisted as they wanted to know what "examinations" were and wanted to *know* this through practice. They were given a test and told they had a certain amount of time to complete it. Immediately on receiving the exam, they gathered together and began to discuss the questions and the possible answers, and the reasoning behind each answer. When Lenkersdorf intervened to tell them that sharing answers in that way was not allowed during the taking of exams, they were incredulous and confused. Why couldn't they, as human learners, take the test *together*? Lenkersdorf explained the rules of "Western" educational exams and the reasons they were administered in that way. However, for the Tojolab'al, the very notion of learning in isolation is alien to their way of being and thinking; the idea of testing knowledge without discussing it with others, in community, is simply absurd.

4. Tik and Modern Thought

At its most uncontroversial, the Western humanist tradition tells us that a self is an isolated subjectivity capable of self-constitution in acts of knowing, doing, or feeling (see, for instance, Descartes and Sartre) and that sociality is *one* of its *possible* modalities of being (for instance, Rousseau and Heidegger). According to this tradition, the individual is prior to the community and, in most cases, takes priority over it.

We find this in twentieth century Mexican thought as well. Octavio Paz, for instance, finds a labyrinthine solitude constituting postcolonial and post-Revolutionary Mexican life. The modern Mexican is a solitary being who has forsaken his past and has found refuge in himself.

> Mexicans have renounced their origins. The modern Mexican does not want to be either Indian or Spaniard, nor does he wish to be descended from them. He denies them and he does not affirm himself as a mixture, but rather as an abstraction; he is a man. He becomes the son of nothingness. His beginnings are in his own self. (Paz 1985, 87)

Placing his "beginnings" in his ego, what comes next is community and togetherness. However, Paz, keeping with the Western tradition, nonetheless prioritizes the individual as a ground for what's to come.

The concept of tik stands against the default Western prioritization of individuality favoring, rather, a radical we-ness or us-ness that denies solitude as a prior and primary mode of existence. If one expresses one's opinion, acts on one's own, or accomplishes a personal feat, one does so because of, for the sake of, or with the community. *Concern* for others is always the filter.

As I write these words, the "I" that writes appears somewhat abstract. If the Tojolab'al are right, then it is a "we" that writes, that thinks, that acts. This is a hard thought to have, especially given *my* education, *my* upbringing, *my* cultural conditioning, etc. Moreover, if it is a "we" that writes and thinks these thoughts, to what "we" does my "I" belong? In scientific writing, the general rule is to use "we" so as to capture the group of researchers doing similar work now or in the past; in the humanities, the inclusive we identifies the reader and the writer in some intimate, familiar, way. But these are just conventions. In neither of these cases does one take seriously the idea that "we" are in this together (whatever "this" is!).

What would it mean to adopt a we-framework? It would mean taking seriously those communities of which we are a part. Talk of "intersectionality," for instance, refers to our membership in various communities, and, furthermore, to how these communities constitute us as subjects in common struggle. As such, intersectionality is itself a kind of we-framework, one constituted by a community of communities, one that dislodges the "I" from its privilege the moment one becomes aware of it and of one's belonging in multiple spheres of resistance.

5. Conclusion

The Tojolab'al notion of organic community as tik privileges we-ness and common concern over individuality and the centering of subjective interests. For the sake of others in common, the organic community absorbs subjective interests and subjective power, while never fully rejecting them. There is a self, but it is not more important than the community; there are individual subjects, but they work to complement one another in a common social and existential struggle. As Lenkersdorf (2005) notes, "[c]omplementarity as consensus show that it is about organic units that distinguish themselves qualitatively speaking from the sum of their parts" (115). Allowing the subject to persist means a we-intentionality will always be informed by differing perspectives for the good of the "organic unit." More importantly, however, it means that thought itself, one directed to the care of itself and others in common, namely, philosophy as *care-full consideration*, will rest always already on multiplicity and heterogeneity, or, as Lenkersdorf says, "plurality . . . not only implies subjective difference but directs philosophy to demand diversity" (115).

If we think of a Tojolab'al philosophy as the consequence of this kind of reflection into Tojolab'al thought, we can say that this philosophy is decolonizing in a very specific way. Tik defines a people and *living in it* defines a way of *not* being European. In prioritizing community or us-ness, that is, the Tojolab'al define themselves in opposition to a hegemonic world system bent on marginalizing and alienating non-Western peoples.

Finally, our reflections on tik define a way to unburden ourselves of our adherence to the *ideal* of community. For the Tojolab'al, the organic community is a real, operational, entity that serves as the condition for understanding the cosmos. As the Tojolab'a themselves say, "[tik] is what is distinctive about our culture, our identity, our manner of being" (34). Tik is not a way to relate oneself to the world, it is the only way, and is one that preserves identity, difference, and plurality.

6

The Figure of the World

Overview of the Concept: *What Luis Villoro calls the "figure of the world" refers to a basic way of seeing and interpreting the world—it is what grounds a particular interpretive or cultural framework. The figure of the world can be unique, but also arrogant, to specific cultural or historical standpoints. Colonial reason is grounded on a very Eurocentric, and Christian, figure of the world where only those aspects of the world that resemble it—including other human beings or other belief systems—are understood and allowed. In this sense, colonial reason is a closed, or arrogant, type of reason. Because of the persistence of colonial reason (coloniality) in our own day, understanding and challenging its grounding figure of the world is a required first step in any diversification or decolonization effort.*

In *Analysis of Mexican Being*, Emilio Uranga argues that European reason has established the parameters for evaluating what does and does not count as "human," and it has done so while "arrogantly" proclaiming itself as the standard measure for any such evaluation. In trying to demarcate the civilized from the primitive, the good from the bad, or the accidental from the "substantial," Europeans set themselves apart as non-accidental, appealing to an unwarranted sense of superiority, to what Uranga calls "arrogant substantiality" (107). The notion of arrogant substantiality is left undeveloped by Uranga. However, it anticipates the notion of "arrogant reason," developed by Carlos Pereda half a century later, one that itself refers to the colonial tendency to deny, demean, or bemoan the existence of other rationalities or other modes of existence in an effort to continually reaffirm itself.[1]

This notion is illustrated by Luis Villoro, who relates the subtle, yet catastrophic, ways in which a colonial interpretive framework prevented Europeans from fully appreciating the value and necessity of indigenous humanity and its corresponding cosmologies. These colonial frameworks, Villoro continues, are underpinned by a basic belief structure that is both arrogant and uncompromising; he calls this basic belief structure, the interpretive framework's "figure of the world." The notion of "figure of the world" refers to those bedrock beliefs on which our entire interpretive framework stands; the figure of the world is that which colors the glasses through which we see the world; the figure of the world, that is, sets the boundary limits of what we could alternatively call arrogant substantiality, arrogant reason, or colonial reason.

In this chapter, our focus is on what Villoro calls colonial reason's "figure of the world." While, according to Villoro, the "figure of the world" is the core belief structure of any interpretive framework, we see how in colonial, or arrogant, reason it itself becomes the interpretative framework. We will thus think about how colonial reason's figure of the world contributes to a specific understanding of the other, one that, historically, has motivated the other's dehumanization, objectification, and attempts at eradication.[2]

1. On Colonial Reason

In "Sahagún, or the Limits of the Discovery of the Other," Villoro[3] makes the following observation:

> With America, the West proposes to itself the problem of difference for the first time. It is possible, in principle, to understand the wholly different? What are the limits of that understanding? Can these limits be surpassed? The 16th century in New Spain offers a privileged laboratory for answering these questions. (1999, 16)

Much is revealed in the experiments conducted in this "laboratory." In particular, it is learned that the "limits" of Western "understanding," or alternatively, *colonial reason*, are "surpassed" by "the wholly different." The surpassing of these limits, however, is regarded negatively as a *trespassing*, as a violation, forcing colonial reason to close itself off to the wholly different. Colonial reason thus fortifies itself by doubling down on its own superiority, on its own arrogance, ultimately denying or rejecting the validity and value of the other.

1.1 Lessons from the Laboratory

Villoro's "Sahagún" (1999) locates the arrogance of colonial reason in certain basic assumptions at work during the colonizing project.

Villoro begins by stressing that Western understanding was shocked with the discovery of *another* world besides the one already known and categorized; a shock rooted in the realization that "the world no longer had a center" (15). This de-centering of the world would obviously require social, political, and economic recalibrations, but it would also demand a moral and hermeneutical reckoning that in the sixteenth century, would bring with it "new challenges," including "the necessity to recognize a radical otherness" (15). This was a "challenge" for Western, or colonial, reason, forced as it was to consider the limits of its tolerance and the tolerance of its limits.

From the beginning, colonial reason rested on a key bedrock assumption, one that would make the challenge even more challenging: *true humanity belongs to Western, white, Christian men*. This assumption is historical, and Mexican philosophers in the twentieth century recognized it as the persistent premise of Western reason throughout the centuries. As Uranga (2013) observes: "The truly human belongs to Western history, and from that point of view the supposed humanity of the American [indigenous peoples] is nothing but a 'beastliness'" (164). Said differently, anything not conforming to the "bedrock assumption" or "point of view" of what is "truly human" can only be inhuman, beastly. That "point of view," interpretive framework, or understanding, Uranga points outs, can only distinguish between humans and beasts, seeing as beasts all those that are neither Western nor (white, European) men.

Uranga writes: "Let's not be subtle, if [this is the model of the human] we do not fit in the scheme. Furthermore, the concession of 'humanness' to those who do not speak Greek or Latin [indigenous people] is a clumsy Christianizing maneuver which is both objectionable and *blamable*" (156).

In "Sahagún," Villoro calls the "bedrock assumption" or "point of view" of Western history, colonial reason's "figure of the world." It is colonial reason's "figure of the world" that adjudicated between the human and the beast. Villoro describes the "figure of the world" as the basic, underlying, set of assumptions that *lend a figure, shape, form, and intelligibility to the world.*

> The system of beliefs of every culture is ultimately based on a certain way of seeing the world in accordance with certain basic values and categories. Before each culture, the world "configures itself" in a specific way. Let us call these basic beliefs, which ground all others, the "figure of the world." The figure of the world is, in each culture, the collective presupposition of any other belief. (Villoro 1999, 16)

We can say that colonial reason grounds itself on and as a specifically Eurocentric *configuration* of the world, or on and as a "figure of the world" that is old, defined, and rigid. Beliefs about indigenous peoples, their customs, traditions, *and* their humanity, are then built on such a foundation. As rigid, this figure of the world will not bend to new information, other configurations, or *other* figures of the world. It is, in this sense, *arrogant*. As arrogant, it will resist alteration, alterity, or *otherness*.

The figure of the world is a product of history, constructed years before the Spanish set foot in America. It was the result of experience with other cultures and other ways of life that were non-European. By the time it arrives in America, it is capable of accommodating, or better yet, tolerating, *some* differences and uniqueness. However, the encounter with the overwhelming complexity of American indigenous civilizations was simply too much to handle. In other words, while the difference was already built into the European figure of the world, some difference was intolerable.

On encountering the American difference, that which they could recognize and tolerate was drowned out by what they could not. The encountered difference appeared incompatible with their figure of the world, it could not be accommodated into their hermeneutical frameworks or existing forms of intelligibility. What was this difference?

First, it was the naked Indians, which appear as coming out of paradise after the first instant of creation. Then, the greatest shock: a strange civilization which pairs the most subtle refinement with the bloodiest cruelty. It resembles nothing known nor does it remind notions already learned. It lacks those elements that seemed to be the conditions for all superior civilization: for example, it does not know steel, the wheel, or the horse. However, it has achieved moral and artistic elevation . . . Order and wisdom coexist with brutal actions which honor frightening rock images. The European does not know if he is before civilization or barbarism . . . The indigenous culture is the "never before seen," the radical other. (16)

Faced with nakedness, brutality, the monstrosity of their art, and heretic and violent religious practices, but at the same time, with artistic refinement, order, and wisdom, "shock" the European mind. As a result, chronicles of the encounter tell the story of the "zozobra" that befell the European, who found himself suddenly overcome with "admiration and horror at the same time" (Villoro 1999, 16).

Finding itself in zozobra, colonial reason reacts and does what reason does, namely, seek to understand the difference and overcome its confusion (overcome its zozobra). This understanding would come with an added plus, something more besides pacifying a reason in zozobra, namely, it would bring about the kind of knowledge benefiting the project of colonization and conquest in which they were involved.

We can't forget that there was an ulterior motive to understanding indigenous language, culture, and practices: dominion over gold, territory, and souls. To this end, that of understanding, they deployed technologies of domination, including translation, transcription, bilingualism, and so on, which facilitated the cataloging of the other for the interest of totalization and domination.

In this context, Villoro articulates what we can call the *domination thesis*. He writes,

> It is not possible to deal with others without understanding them. This is more certain if the goal is to dominate them. The need to understand the alien culture is born from a will to dominate. (16)

The domination thesis is ultimately internal to the colonial figure of the world; the domination thesis is the heart of colonial figure of the world.

The question now has to do with *how* colonial reason confronts, and ultimately consumes, difference and *why*. Let's look at that now.

1.2 Moments of Colonial Reason

Villoro differentiates the colonial understanding of the other into three moments, each moment representing a horizon of intelligibility within which the indigenous other could (or can) be understood. These moments can be characterized in the following way:

(1) Objectification: the other is an object of colonial reason.
(2) Assimilation: the other is reduced to the categories of colonial reason.
(3) Annihilation: the other proves radically incompatible with colonial reason.

These "moments" are not sequential. The other can be understood within the horizon of the third moment without having been first understood within the horizon of the second. Nor does the understanding, in exhausting itself in one, move on to the next; it may simply remain there. The other can be understood within the horizon of the first moment permanently—one's effort at understanding another can permanently remain at the level of assimilation or, when intolerant, at the level of annihilation, *seeking to destroy what reason cannot understand.*

Each of these moments, however, contains a possibility of radical understanding; this is the overcoming of the limits of the moment. In other words, overcoming the limits of the first moment would mean that the other has been acknowledged as different, as a subject; overcoming the limits of the second would be to affirm that difference as valuable in its own right; and to go beyond the limits of the third would be to respect that difference and allow it to exist (perhaps worthy of adoption or even imitation). However, this overcoming is precluded by colonial reason's figure of the world, that is, the domination thesis.

1.2.1 First Moment: Objectification

The moments indicated earlier refer to the different ways in which the other can be grasped and understood within the horizon of intelligibility afforded by colonial reason's figure of the world. These moments are either lived simultaneously or are spread out in time. Villoro illustrates how this is so by appealing to the history of the conquest of the Valley of Mexico, where the actual or historical encounter is temporally differentiated. The first moment is illustrated by the manner in which the other appears to the European (to colonial reason) as an object among objects (a creature among creatures, among trees, with other animals, etc.). This is the moment of objectification. Villoro (1999) writes:

> the first moment of understanding the other consists in conjoining its otherness, that is, in translating that otherness in terms of familiar objects and situations from our own world, capable of falling under known values and categories, within the horizon of our picture of the world . . . eliminating difference in this way. (16)

We notice the domination thesis at work here; this first moment already involves *dehumanization*. The other is "translated" into a term in the framework of colonial reason, namely, the indigenous other is an object among objects. What is seen is interpreted in accordance with what is already known to European or colonial reason, with what is familiar, and with what fits the figure of the world. This reduction goes like this: "The American infidels are assimilated to the Moors . . . a 'cacique' is a king . . . a 'Tlatoani' is an emperor in the Roman style, an Aztec temple is a mosque, its idols, Moloch, its cities, new Venices or new Sevilles" (Villoro 1999, 16).

Of course, this reduction to the familiar, this erasure of difference, is only effective until the other resists its own objectification. While the European interpretive framework seeks to assimilate the difference it encounters, there are differences that don't easily give themselves to assimilation or reduction. Villoro puts it thus:

> But the analogy with known terms has its limits. There are characteristics of the alien culture which are deep and resist being placed below familiar categories, since they do not fit within the figure of the subject's figure of the world, which establishes the horizon and the limits of the understandable. Those non-translatable aspects constitute, then, the negative par excellence. Moreover, since they are outside our own figure of the world, they have to be judged either as prior to all culture and history or as that which contradicts and negates culture. In this way, interpretation oscillates between extremes. In one, the Indian in his alterity is seen as a natural being, an Adam, prior to the establishment of any sort of republic, and, as such, of any sort of history. He is the innocent that ignores sin but also science and law. (16–17)

Ultimately, indigenous difference places great stress on Western interpretive frameworks. The characteristic arrogance of colonial reason is challenged here by unwieldy and ungraspable (via known concepts) otherness, and it reacts by redefining what it sees as "the negative par excellence," that is, as what is inferior to it or as its greatest threat. Incapable of retrofitting the framework in order to allow the other to *co-exist* in its unfamiliarity, they must be judged and relocated to a different conceptual scheme: either, the other as "prior to all culture and history" (i.e., as prehistorical primitives, barbarians) or as that "which contradicts and negates all culture."

Christian missionaries understood the indigenous other in the first sense, as childlike, and thus needing salvation; others, like Hernan Cortez, understood them in the second sense, as the contradiction of everything they believed, as the "contrary" of their *figure of the world*, namely, as irreconcilable and Satanic. In both cases, the other does not cohere with the picture of humanity inherent to colonial reason, a picture in which European humanity is complete and beyond reproach; in simple terms, the other is rejected by the *arrogance* of colonial reason. As Villoro puts it: "The basic belief system of the West makes it clear [*establece*] that there can be only one truth and only one human destiny" (17). This is arrogant reason:

> if any other culture pretends to have another truth or another destiny it negates our figure of the world. It can be understood only as pure negativity. The other is darkness and hiddenness, that which says "no" to the world, the demonic . . . it is, by definition, what cannot be integrated into our world and it deserves to be destroyed. (17)

Arrogant colonial reason will not budge. Rather than accept or respect difference, it will simply redefine what it sees in terms it can nicely fit back into its own scheme. Villoro concludes this section by reminding us that for the Western reason the indigenous other existed only as an object for the European subject. He writes:

> The voice of the other can only be heard to the extent that it coheres with our concepts and values, those commonly accepted by our society, because the real world can only have meanings that do not differ from the ones given to it by the only valid subject, the Western subject. (17)

1.2.2 Second Moment: Assimilation

In the first moment, colonial reason *objectifies* the indigenous other. The other is understood only as an object for a subject, is made comprehensible when it is reduced to what is already known, to what is familiar, and nonthreatening. However, because the indigenous other resists this initial objectification as a mere object among objects (perhaps by speaking, building, or worshiping), the objectification switches gear while still working within its horizon of intelligibility. The indigenous other is objectified now as either belonging to primitive humanity or, due to its non-Christian way of life, as demonic.

Understanding others as either barbarians or demonic, however, limits the scope of interaction and sociality so much so that for the European conquerors, it threatened the evangelizing mission. How can the *Christian* empire expand when there are no souls to save, no intelligences bearing witness to the Good News? The European figure of the world, and colonial reason generally, needed to adapt, perhaps expand, in order to allow a new level of understanding the other.

The *second moment* in the understanding of the other thus involves a minimal humanization. The interpretive framework allows the endowment of enough humanity to make *assimilation* into the Christian faith possible. This minimal humanization of the indigenous other, however, depends on reimagining the indigenous other via abstract, Christian notions of a soul-bearing subject—that is, as capable of having salvageable souls and therefore of being converted and baptized.

According to Villoro (1999), it was Bartolomé de las Casas who best exemplified colonial reason's second moment: "[de las Casas] asks that we listen to the other, that we hear his voice. This is the first recognition of the other as subject" (18). But listening to the other, or hearing the other's voice, does not yet mean that the other is *respected*. This is especially the case if, when listening, the other is continually interrupted by the urgency of the Christian message. Sure, at this moment of understanding, the other is *recognized* in its otherness and difference, but only for ends benefiting the evangelizing mission; she is still not allowed to embody and live that difference.

In this second moment, Villoro continues, the figure of the world contains "principles that allow one to judge the other as equal" (18), including the following: "All men are children of God, all are free, rational, regardless of how different they may seem. They all have, before the Law of Peoples and Divine Designs, the same rights. The other is thus not reduced to a mere object there for exploitation" (18). However, there's a catch to such humanization, namely, that the reason for bestowing it is so that those gifted with humanity may be baptized. At this level, the other's otherness is only recognized to the extent that it can be reduced and replaced with that which is familiar, a soul capable of being converted. Villoro says that at this level, colonial reason fails to "go past the picture of the world that includes the basic belief in Providence as what gives meaning to history" (18). Ultimately, the indigenous other is humanized only so that she may freely choose to accept the European version of the world—that is, humanized in accordance with the domination thesis and the colonial figure of the world. As Villoro puts it, "[d]ialogue only admits the other as equal so that he can voluntarily choose the values of the one who knows the true sense of history" (18–19).

In the end, even those most tolerant of difference could not accept the radical alterity that the indigenous other represented, as was the case with Bartolomé de las Casas. Villoro proposes that "de las Casas could not admit the possibility of multiple truths" (18)—the truth of the indigenous others and his own, Christian, truth. The only option, then, is assimilation of that other truth into one's own, which means that it must be stripped of its difference and subsumed into one's own. So, yes, we may allow the other to speak her truth, but if her truth does not confirm or conform to my truth, then her truth is no truth at all—moreover, within the horizon of colonial reason, it is blasphemy! While de las Casas accepts the indigenous other as his equal and believes they should have rights as human beings, his interpretive frameworks cannot sustain the indigenous difference, and this because "de las Casas is incapable of conceiving a different interpretation of a world different than his own" (25).

1.2.3 Third Moment: Annihilation

The third moment in the understanding of the is phrased entirely as a hypothetical. Villoro (1999) writes:

> The possibility remains for a third level in the understanding of the other. This would be the recognition of the other in her equality and in her diversity. It would be to recognize her in with the same sense that she herself gives to her world. [With the conquerors and colonizers] this level was never reached. However, there were some who caught a glimpse of it, only to immediately retreat. The first and most notable was Friar Bernardino de Sahagún. He opened a window and found himself before the other's gaze, but he could not see himself in that gaze. (19)

At this moment, colonial reason *could* recognize the other in "equality" and "diversity" and respect. This "recognition" of diversity or difference would mean that the other is understood by colonial reason as she understands herself and/in her world. While at the *second moment* the other is understood in her familiarity and sameness so as to be assimilated to the colonial figure of the world, at this level, understanding her unfamiliarity or diversity would mean letting go of the temptation to assimilate, allowing her be, and accepting her *as other*. However, this moment is only an ideal or "possibility" that was "never reached" by Europeans. According to Villoro, only the Franciscan friar, Bernardino de Sahagún (1499–1590) was able to recognize the possibility before correcting himself; Sahagún came close, but stopped short of undermining his own Christian faith (his figure of the world).

Arriving in Mexico eight years after Conquest (1529), "Sahagún was the first to attentively listen to the Indian and to systematically give him the word" (19). Sahagún engaged indigenous others in dialogue, as equals. He asked the elders to tell him about their culture, art, what they did before the arrival of the Spanish, their beliefs, and their rites. Significantly, he asked them to do so in their own language and learned how to speak and write Nahual. It is at this moment, historically, when, "[f]inally, the other has the word, his own word. It is the Christian who now listens" (19). From this encounter, Sahagún *learns* the extent of the sophistication and complexity of the indigenous worldview; more importantly, he *learns* that their moral, political, and religious systems are not factually inferior to his own.

What impresses Sahagún most of all is the rigorous moral codes to which his indigenous interlocutors subscribe to:

> Sahagún describes the strength that constructs and nourishes that society: an ascetic and rigorous education capable of dominating the natural inclinations and edifying a virtuous republic. That society rested, above all, on the cultivation of one virtue: fortitude, "that which among them was esteemed more than any other and on which they could climb to the highest level of value." (Villoro 1999, 19–20)

Knowing these sophisticated moral codes and practices, Sahagún comes to admire and respect indigenous reason. However, his respect is rooted not on something independently good about that *other* reason, but rather, it is rooted in the fact that Sahagún reads indigenous ethics, politics, and religion through his own Christian interpretive framework and, in this way, finds them complimentary in significant ways. For instance, like Christians, the Nahual-speaking people practiced and taught humility, temperance, chastity, a love of work, respect for family and community, honesty, and a love of God. As Villoro puts it, "[the indigenous] moral code was based on fortitude and austerity, and maintained thanks to kind of justice that was inflexible and proven, the example of a noble and righteous nobility, and capable of representing itself as a model for all the people. Their republic had been, Sahagún believes, governed by the strong and the wise" (20). Moreover, their highest God possessed "attributes closer to the Christian God than did the god of the pagans" (21). In Nahual mythology, god "was the creator of heaven and earth, all powerful, invisible . . . he was everywhere" (20). For Sahagún, this sounded all-too familiar.

While the practice of human sacrifice was morally and religiously objectionable, indigenous views on moral conduct and their concept of God meant that they were not only capable of profound spiritual commitment but ethically sophisticated. *The problem*, however, was simple: their religious views, and the moral codes that flowed from them, as admirable as they were, *were not Christian*. With this problem at hand the decision is whether or not to allow indigenous reason to exist *alongside* Christian/Western/colonial reason. Of course, the domination thesis at the heart of the colonial figure of the world will not allow such coexistence. Rather than change *his* most fundamental beliefs (his figure of the world), Sahagún, for his own sake and in the name of his divine office, must agree that the "fascinating" yet accidental world has to be corrected or, if impervious to correction, eradicated.

Sahagún was willing to know the ways of the other, to respect their practices and beliefs; however, he was incapable of going beyond the bounds of colonial reason and accept that the indigenous way of life represented *another* way to live. He couldn't accept this other way because the figure of the world represented by indigenous reason lacked that which was most fundamental to his own, namely, "Truth," or Christ. Thus, indigenous reason, in lacking *the Truth*, was not itself true, valid, or worthy of preservation. Indigenous reason fell short because it did *not yet know* Christ—something that *could* be corrected with time and philosophy. Villoro describes the breaking point:

> Sahagun can admit the discourse of the other until a certain point: until the moment in which he must deny the basic belief that lends sense to his own life and the presence of Christianity in America. He cannot deny what the other shows, but neither can he deny his own interpretation of the world, one which constitutes him. He must then conjugate the vision of the world that the other presents him so that he may include it in his own. His solution is a doubling [*un desdoblamiento*]. (22)

Sahagún's "solution" is to acknowledge that there are two ways to see and understand the world. One way is the correct way, the other is the incorrect way. This "doubling" of reason is meant to set up European, colonial, reason as the best alternative. While there was much that Sahagún appreciated about indigenous reason, much that he admired because he found it similar to his own Christian worldview, without Christ at its center indigenous theology was simply too worldly. This meant that what "in the eyes of the indigenous person were gods, to the European [they] were demons" (22). This "doubling" sought then to present to the indigenous other an "opposing criterion of truth," a *divine* opposed to a *demonic* option, its "antithesis" (22). Consequently, "in an effort to save his own figure of the world, Sahagún declares the indigenous picture of the world an appearance, and that which is revealed by Scripture reality" (23).

Here and in other colonial contexts, the practice of "doubling" is a practice of separating and distancing elements of the indigenous world, including its models of understanding, into the realm of absolute, irreconcilable difference. It is, in effect, a key moment in the practice of domination, as the difference is claimed to be *known* yet untrue or invalid, and hence unworthy of independence or existence. For Sahagún, what he experienced in his confrontations with the indigenous other—their humanity, their moral fortitude, and so on—was not enough to override the arrogance of colonial reason.

The problem with arrogant colonial reason and its figure of the world is that it is resistant to difference. What it does not already include, it does not see. As Villoro puts it: "[Sahagún] opened the window and found himself captured by the other's gaze; however, he could not see himself in that gaze" (19). Sahagún came closest to breaking through the third moment of colonial reason. In a sense, his effort at listening and speaking with the indigenous other represents the moment at which others are either recognized and accepted in their truth and difference or one's own reason, in recognizing its own limits, position, and arrogance, seeks the other's annihilation. More often than not, this is the moment where the reality of another way of life, another world and another reason, is seen clearly for what it is, in all of its diversity, and found to be overly abounding, profound, and vast to fit into one's set conception of the world; it is at this moment that that other reason must be denied or rejected. Put another way, at this (third) level, knowing and recognizing is not an opening into valuing the other. That difference that the other represents (which gives him his value) is irreconcilable and, as with his idols or his temples, must be smashed to pieces.

2. A Figure of the World

We began with Emilio Uranga, who decries the narcissism of a Western humanism that suggests that its conceptions of personhood are the standard measure. This is a kind of rational narcissism where Europeans reserve the very *substance* of humanity for themselves while colonized or marginalized peoples are mere properties—in both senses of this term—of that substance. Uranga calls this "arrogant substantiality," which we are also calling *arrogant* colonial reason.

Villoro sees the arrogance of colonial reason manifested as Europeans impose their figure of the world on indigenous culture, life, and reason. This imposition seemed necessary, especially for Sahagún, since in "doubling" reason, only one option was godly, while the other demonic. It seemed even more necessary because European identity was at stake. Because the figure of the world refers to those basic, underlying assumptions that structure identity relations with the world and with others, to allow these basic, underlying assumptions to change would require re-structuring one's identity itself.

The figure of the world is thus more than a mere framework of intelligibility. It is what we believe and what we are. The basic beliefs that make it up refer back to ourselves, to who we are and what we value. Villoro says:

> The picture of the world has a vital function, not only theoretical but also vital. It involves . . . meaning and ultimate values. To negate it . . . would be to annul [our] own identity . . . it would be to renounce the global project that lends meaning to [our] life. (24)

The figure of the world is thus a core belief structure. For Europeans, it was the engine driving colonial reason in its confrontation with the indigenous other. This engine was fueled by the domination thesis, and it represented "the final ideological remainder that impedes the full recognition of the other, both as equal and at the same time as different" (Villoro 1999, 26).

So what do we make of Sahagún's efforts at understanding his indigenous interlocutors? Ultimately, the project of understanding the other is another weapon in the arsenal of domination. Colonial reason serves as the justification for interpreting the other in a way that would un-realize him, transforming him into a manageable resource. "The other can only be understood in so far as his subjectivity is denied and he is reduced to a determinate object by the categories of the European. It is then that the other can be dominated" (25). Sahagún toyed with the idea of allowing the other to reveal his difference in his own words, stretching the limits colonial reason itself. But colonial reason recoiled at the notion, threatened by the all-too-human voice of the other. As Villoro puts it: "There is nothing more dangerous than allowing the other to speak when the goal is to dominate him" (25).

3. Challenging Arrogance

Sahagún's colonial rationality, which rested on a vital, yet arrogant, picture of the world, would ultimately not allow him to accept the radical difference that the other represented. It was, in the last instance, a rationality of exclusion, erasure, and domination. But his is not an isolated historical problem.

Today, each of us is nailed into place by our figure of the world, one we share with others in our culture, with others in our milieu, and which is reflected in our ideological commitments and in our philosophy. In this way, Anglo-American culture restricts itself by a rigid, that is, arrogant, rationality that marginalizes other rationalities, other figures of the world, into peripheries and inhuman spaces. And all this, because, as Villoro puts it, its "figure of the world cannot be surpassed" (25), which means that in its arrogance, it is incapable of understanding difference.

Villoro recommends a challenge to our entrenchment in arrogant, colonial reason. The challenge is to allow *ourselves to be seen and changed by other reasons and other pictures of the world*. This exposing of ourselves in the gaze of the other is the entryway into destabilizing our own ideological frameworks and more than simply tolerating the other, accepting them in their full difference. Villoro (1999) writes:

> Only a figure of the world that admits of the plurality of reason and meaning can understand both equality and diversity of subjects. To recognize the validity of that which is equal and different to us is to renounce any previous idea to dominate, it is to lose the fear of discovering ourselves, equal and diverse, in the gaze of the other. Is this possible? I don't know. But, however, only in that sense would it be possible to replace forever the danger of man's destruction by man,

only that change would allow one to elevate to a superior level human history. (26)

This, of course, means that we allow ourselves to be changed in a fundamental way by that which is different. Our figure of the world will change in the confrontation with another only if we "admit" the other's difference and "renounce" our will to dominate. This requires, however, something more than toleration or humility, and Villoro "doesn't know" what this would be. But he has an idea:

> It could only be possible if we began with a basic belief that accepted, from the start, that reason is plural, that truth and meaning are not discoverable from a privileged point of view but can be accessible to other infinities, that the world can be understood beginning from different paradigms. For that, one would have to accept a reality essentially plural, as much as from the different manner in which it "configures" itself before man, as from the different values that give it sense. One would have to break with the idea, specific to the entire history of Europe, that history has a center. In a plural world, any subject is the center. (26)

Recently, Carlos Pereda (2019) has proposed that an effective countermeasure to arrogance is "self-interruption," whereby we "interrupt our customary reactions" to what confronts us and "allow ourselves to be overtaken by feelings of astonishment, incomprehension and pain" (25). Pereda calls this a "difficult and infuriating art" (25), suggesting that it takes practice, patience, and empathy. Applied to Sahagún, the idea is that if he would have practiced self-interruption, he would have been able to empathize with the indigenous other in a more visceral way. He would have been able to *hear and feel them* and, in a certain way, punctured the thick protective layer of his arrogant colonial reason. Ultimately, Pereda (2020) suggests that the art of self-interruption begins to dissolve the layers of arrogant reason, leading to, what he calls, "porous reason," in which one comes to "at times doubt even one's most cherished evaluative schemes with the purpose of detoxifying oneself [of them] and [likewise] of one's social inheritance: of cultivating gaps in one's own *power* so as to hear other voices" (252).

In the end, Sahagún cannot detoxify himself from the arrogant normative prescriptions of colonial reason. It was too much to ask, it seems, from a Christian missionary in the sixteenth century seeking to further the evangelizing mission. But Villoro thinks it is not too late for us. Anticipating Pereda, he proposes that we can overcome the arrogance of our reason if we accept that there is more than one way to experience and make sense of the world; if we accept that there is a plurality of reason (what Pereda calls "porous reason").

In the last instance, Villoro teaches us that the process of knowing the other is always informed by ideological interests—that care must be taken that we are not seeking to dominate that which we do not fully understand. In a more significant way, he asks us to consider that our basic beliefs (our figure of the world) may be so arrogant that we fail to see ourselves as closed off to others and other ways of seeing the world. It is thus not the case that beyond our specific figure of the world, beyond the limits of our reason, there is nothing; it is not the case that beyond the horizon there is the unthinkable, the unwieldy, the strange, or the dangerous. Allowing the destabilization, fracture, and fragmentation of our ways to think about the world means that we can rethink the world and the other, not as objects, reflections of ourselves, or inaccessible curiosities, but as ends in themselves, mysteries wholly capable of enriching my life and my world while bringing me closer to an incomprehensible givenness closer to mysticism than domination.

4. Reintroduction

A number of years ago I found myself struggling to write a closing chapter for my dissertation on what I called at that time, "phenomenological epistemology." The work tried to make sense of the German philosopher Edmund Husserl's theory of justification, and in the last chapter I wanted to accomplish two things: one, to show in a clear and concise way that my reading was different, and two, to suggest that *other* non-German, non-French, or non-Anglo philosophers had equally grappled with Husserl's phenomenology in similarly unorthodox ways. The first was easy as all I had to do was conjure up a familiar scene of someone seeking to justify their beliefs in the way explained in the dissertation. The second was more difficult for two reasons: the first was that I was not initially aware of *any* of these "others" and finding them would be challenging, and the second was that when I did find them, I could not *allow myself* to *read* them as contributing anything different, original, or meaningful to the discourse. It was as if there was an internal block that prevented me from accepting that a Latin American phenomenologist could say something that had not been said before by the Gadamers, Finks, or Derridas of the world. I ended up with a chapter on Husserl and Ortega y Gasset that while still valuable, left me deeply unsatisfied.

The day I submitted my dissertation I grabbed some books that I had neglected for a few years and headed to a bar to decompress and celebrate. I settled in and opened the first: Jorge Portilla's *La fenomenología del relajo*. This moment would change the trajectory of my professional life, as I would dedicate the next fifteen years to Mexican philosophy while completely ignoring Husserl and phenomenological epistemology. But as I sat there then, I wondered *why had I not read this book before?* I wondered also *why I had struggled with the last chapter of the dissertation?* In fact, that which had prevented me from imagining what to include in the last chapter was related to the *reason* as to why I had never read Portilla. But what was that relation? At the root of it was the fact that Portilla *could not be* counted as a suitable subject for a chapter on the history of phenomenology. Why? First, because, according to Western reason, the Western history of philosophy is complete, it is historical, and because it is complete and historical, it is superior (I would later learn that a philosophy which is *other* to that history challenges its completeness, the validity of its history, and its superiority). As comfortable as I was with *my* historical account of phenomenology, allowing this other history to intervene would have been devastating, if only for its practical consequences (dissertation deadlines, fellowships, advisers, etc.). And second, because what Portilla was contributing was not "philosophical," according to the history of philosophy to which I subscribed (halfheartedly, but arrogantly, nonetheless).

The "truth" is that a colonial framework scaffolds the Western history of philosophy. This is reflected in an existent ontology of marginalization or erasure; built into that colonial framework, that is, is the necessary marginalization of other ways of looking at the world. This explains the *uncanny* feeling one gets when talking about, for example, Jorge Portilla's notion of "seriousness" without mentioning Jean-Paul Sarte; or why it feels *weird* to talk about Villoro's "figure of the world" without talking about Gadamer's theory of interpretation, and so on. What I've realized is that my "uncanny" and "weird" feelings are colonial reasons telling me that neither Portilla nor Villoro is *necessary* (although Sarte and Gadamer *are*). As we've seen, this is colonial reason's modus operandi and makes no room for variation, and seeks to reject difference at every turn.

In my case, I was arrogantly tied to the history of philosophy that I had been taught, and any deviation was unacceptable—even as I *wanted* to accept it, even as I hated myself for not accepting it. I was held hostage by the arrogance of Western reason and the Western history of philosophy that represented it. Breaking free would take years and, in a sense, I'm not yet free—you can see signs of that in this book—I'm on parole, working to make a case that there are other reasons, other pictures of the world, and other ways to think philosophy that are equally valid and worthy of our time.

7

Mexistentialism

Overview of the Concept: *Mexistentialism is shorthand for Mexican existentialism. It locates the human struggle in a geographically determined space and historically determined time, both of which affect our being human in a definite way. It concerns itself with the specificity of where and when one happens to find oneself. Mexistentialism's where is Mexico, while its when is postcolonial, and particularly, post-revolutionary Mexico. Mexistentialism is circumstantial, or situational.*

"After all," writes Leopoldo Zea (2017), "if we are to be faithful to [philosophy], we have to affirm that our *situation* is not that of Jean-Paul Sartre. Our situation is not that of the European bourgeoisie" (137).

The Mexico of Mexistentialism's concern is a historical accident of Europe struggling to find both its geopolitical and philosophical identity 500 years after the Conquest. The Mexican subject (*el mexicano*) reflects this "accidentality" and this struggle in its everydayness, contending with "nepantla" and "zozobra" as a way of life (*lo mexicano*). Mexistentialism asserts that *the Mexican struggle is a human struggle* but in a specific and particular sense and not in any abstract or universal sense. Conversely, it insists that the *human struggle reflects the Mexican struggle*, insisting that *human existence is Mexican existence*, but not because of some arrogant relativism that says that *all-there-is* is Mexican existence, but because existing becomes significant or meaningful only to the one who experiences it, in this case, for Mexicans thinking about existence.

Elsewhere (2019b) I have referred to this Mexican version of existentialism as (M)existentialism, with parenthesis on the "M" so as to highlight its otherness to European existentialist traditions. That parenthesis, however, indicates a marginalization, suppression, or silencing of the Mexican contributions to this tradition, understood globally. At this time, I remove the parenthesis and signal the end of Mexican existentialism's parenthetical existence.

1. History

Luis Villoro's "Genesis and Task of Existentialism in Mexico" (1949) credits the introduction of existentialism as a *literary* tradition to the Mexican philosopher Antonio Caso (1883–1946), who offers a course on Søren Kierkegaard and the Russian existentialist, Nicolai Berdiaeff in the fall of 1939. However, the arrival of existentialism as a *philosophical* tradition is credited to José Gaos, through whom "the name Heidegger is announced for the first time in Mexico toward the end of the 1930s" (236). According to Villoro, "[i]n the span of five years (between 1942-47), [Gaos] offers courses on *Being and Time*, courses that until today give a systematic exposition of his philosophy" (236). Villoro observes: "[f]ew academic courses had left to that point such a profound imprint in Mexico than those give 'Heideggerian' years. Ever since then there is a surge in interest for existential philosophy" (236).

We thus locate the origins of "Mexistentialism" with Gaos and his courses on Heidegger. However, at the same time in Mexico City, there is also a surge of interest in the broader tradition of existentialism as introduced by Spanish *transterrados* in the late 1930s and early 1940s—*transterrados*, or "transplants," were refugees and exiles fleeing the Spanish Civil War between 1936 and 1939. The list of transterrados is long, but it includes Joaquin Xírau, José Gaos, Juan-David García Baca, Eduardo Nicol, and Maria Zambrano among others (Pereda 2013, 278–9).

Without a doubt, the transterrado with the most impact is Gaos, a former student and assistant to the great Spanish philosopher, José Ortega y Gasset. Villoro points out that in the early 1940s, it is Gaos that introduces Heidegger's *Being and Time* to a new generation of Mexican philosophers (Gaos is also the first to translate *Being and Time*, publishing the first sections in the early 1940s and the complete Spanish translation, *El Ser y el Tiempo*, in 1951). Gaos promotes Heidegger's existential hermeneutic as representing "a guide for the authentic life" (Romanell 1952, 181).

It is in understanding *Being and Time* as a "guide" that we find its initial appeal to young post-Revolutionary, postcolonial Mexicans in search of their own way, represented most notably by "el grupo Hiperión," or the philosophical group "Hyperion." Hyperion found in Heidegger's existentialism a manual both for life and for philosophy, one that would allow them to propose as philosophical their own historically situated thinking.

With Heidegger's *Being and Time* as a manual or guide, Mexican philosophers could justify the value of their own, unique, standpoint or circumstance, especially in regard to their philosophizing. This was, after all, a circumstance that was uniquely theirs and belonged to them in a very specific and intimate way; an existential reality possessing what Heidegger, in *Being and Time* Heidegger, calls "*Jemeinigkeit*" or "mineness" (Heidegger 1962, 68).

However, although their reading of Heidegger allowed them to reserve for themselves a philosophical origin that was theirs and theirs alone, toward the end of the 1940s allegiances shift to French existentialism, and in particular, to the existentialist philosophy of Jean-Paul Sartre, Gabriel Marcel, and Maurice Merleau-Ponty (Uranga 2013, 173). This new allegiance is announced through a series of lectures delivered by Hyperion 1947–8 that paired French existentialism with what most concerned the new Mexican generation, namely, the question "What does it mean to be Mexican?" This question came to embody what has come to be known as "la filosofía de lo mexicano," or *the philosophy of Mexicanness*, a philosophical project that, in general, sought to make sense of *how* history had framed Mexican identity (see Hurtado 2006; Sánchez 2016).

There is great significance to the shift from German to French existentialism, as it represents a reframing of philosophy away from abstract or conceptual considerations—central to Heidegger—and toward the most pressing social, cultural, and existential needs of a people—central to, for instance, the later Sartre or Merleau-Ponty. According to Emilio Uranga (1948):

> Definitively, what decides the value of existentialism is its capacity to lend ground to a systematic description of human existence, but not of human existence in the abstract, but of a situated human existence, in a situation, of a human existence located in a determinate geographic *habitat*, in a social and cultural space also determined and with a precise historical legacy. (240)

This shift thus records a moment in the history of Mexican philosophy when philosophers made a conscious decision to avoid abstractness in favor of descriptions more responsive to the needs and urgencies of their "determinate geographic habitat." For this reason, Heidegger had to go, or, more precisely, he had to be overcome. Heidegger's overcoming is recorded in Uranga's short essay, "Two Existentialisms," where he writes that whereas the initial allure of "existentialism had been amongst us . . . a way of talking about Martin Heidegger" (2013, 173), this quickly changed to a way of talking about Mexico itself. While the phenomenological existentialism of Heidegger, with its focus on temporality and being-in-the-world had cleared the way into a philosophical appreciation of Mexico's own history and circumstance, its abstractness and technicality lent it an *arrogance* that encouraged a sort of colonial prejudice about the nature of philosophy and the philosophical—if it wasn't "serious" or "technical" like Heidegger's then it wasn't philosophy, but, worse, if it wasn't "Heideggerian," then it wasn't existentialism. A more serious reason for Heidegger's overcoming, however, had to do with ethics, or, more specifically, with his apparent *lack* of an ethical stance in *Being and Time*. Uranga (2013) writes: "For my generation, more concretely, for the 'Hiperión' group, what really matters is to know how Sartre deals with moral themes and not with how Heidegger will identify Being or Nothingness in his work" (175). And this, because, the question of morality—the question dealing with human conduct and the good life—"involves consequences which are of much greater and vital importance than those proposed by Heidegger" (175).

What Uranga calls "the value of existentialism" is reaffirmed by Villoro (1949) when he writes:

> The appearance and acceptance of existentialism amongst us responds to a concrete situation that we can only understand if we take into account its temporal dimensions: its projection toward the future and its overcoming negation of the past . . . The yesterday that we encounter will be *our* yesterday. (233)

Again, Villoro's, or Uranga's, "acceptance" of existentialism is not a mere passive adoption of a ready-made philosophical program (as was Positivism in the nineteenth-century or Analytic philosophy in the late twentieth century), but a conscious and active appropriation for the sake, and in the name, of Mexican life. It is in this context, and within this historical framework, that we may talk about "Mexistentialism," a philosophical stance that although remaining faithful to basic existentialists tenets regarding existence, freedom, and finitude, seeks to be more than an abstract philosophical program. We can say that Mexican appropriation was more than academic; it was the effort to put philosophy to work for the Mexican circumstance.

This is but a brief history of existentialism's appearance in Mexico and the ways in which it was appropriated, sublated, and hybridized by Mexican philosophers in the mid-twentieth century. Of course, much more can be said in favor of the argumentative rigor of existentialism in Sartre or Merleau-Ponty, or its elegance in Camus, or the technical wizardry of Heidegger, but Mexican philosophers found its value not in the elegance, rigor, or wizardry of those articulations, but in how, as a philosophical approach to reality, it made possible a description of *their* "situation," *their* "habitat," or *their* "precise historical legacy." This is another way to say that the real value of existentialism is that it can help make sense of existence *wherever* and *whenever* that existence happens to find itself, regardless of its circumstance, habitat, or historical accident. We could call it a nepantla existentialism, as it refuses to settle and easily moves between traditions; however, I'm calling it "Mexistentialism" (without paranthesis) so as to preserve its origin and its difference.

2. Characteristics

My not-so-secret aim is to insert Mexistentialism into the standard history of existentialism, disorienting that history and unsettling our efforts to tell it as we've been telling it. Thus far I've not given much of a reason to suspect that Mexistentialism is disorienting in this way or that it contributes anything significantly new or unique to that standard existentialist story. As we will now see, while Mexistentialism appropriates and traffics in the standard notions of European existentialism, it enriches the existing conceptual archive with notions that, because they are derived from the Mexican struggle or Mexican experience, should unsettle our efforts to tell that standard story as we've been telling it. We are familiar, of course, with the conceptual horizon of European existentialism, one in which we find the notions of freedom, thrownness, anxiety, responsibility, death, subjectivity, faith, absurdity, and boredom. To these, Mexistentialism adds accidentality, insufficiency, zozobra, and nepantla, while confronting and analyzing concepts such as freedom, responsibility, humanism, culture, and death. Let's briefly consider these.

2.1 *Accidentality*

In a superficial sense, accidentality refers to the manner in which human beings are set in relation to that place in the world that they occupy, namely, in a relation of dependence, contingency, or chance. In a more profound sense, accidentality refers to the manner in which human beings are set in relation to *being* itself, likewise in a relation of dependence, contingency, chance, but also insufficiency, deficiency, or lack.

History reveals Mexico, as a nation, to be accidental to the Spanish colonial project. It reveals its people as contingent byproducts of colonization, its culture as reliant on European culture, and the Mexican mestizo ways of life (Mexican "being") as always already insufficient in relation to European *and* indigenous ways of life. In everyday life, Mexicans, either by corazonada or explicitly, "know" this and live with the knowledge of their accidental introduction into world history.

However, a central anti-colonialist claim of Uranga's *Analysis of Mexican Being* is that being accidental is not a *deficiency* of the Mexican given her history, but rather, that deficiency is the authentic, or actual, situation of being human and not just of being Mexican. Uranga concludes, in fact, that *to be human* is to be always insufficient, always dependent, always unnecessary, always accidental.[1] Uranga (2021) says that, as accidental, being human itself is a "minus of being" (103). And there's more:

> The accident is fragility: oscillation between being and nothingness. This means that its "fit" in being, its adhesion to being expressed in the modality of being-in, is not protected by an inalienable right, but rather whatever may be the form of its inherence, it is always revocable. The accident is constantly threatened by displacement [*desalojamiento*]. Attached to being, it can always be torn off from its "there," exterminated. Whatever it holds on to, whatever handle it grabs on to, can be removed. It was born to be-in and at the same time to not-be-in. (116)

The insecurity of being is manifested psychologically in the view that life seems to be constantly slipping away, in the knowledge that whatever we possess is revocable, and that the whole of reality is itself threatening and overwhelming. In an ontological sense, this lack of security points to a fragility and vulnerability that describes us all.

2.2 *Insufficiency*

To be accidental is to be insufficient. Insufficiency is a relational term, pointing to how one fundamentally exists in relation to both the idea of perfection or substance and to others who represent these.

In the history of Mexican philosophy, this fundamental insufficiency has been confused for a superficial complex of inferiority, specifically by Samuel Ramos in his *Profile of Man and Culture in Mexico* of 1934. There, inferiority explains the *psychology* of those who *feel* less than others (Ramos 1962). However, this inferiority, Uranga proposes (against Ramos), is actually a manifestation of insufficiency, and thus not a characteristic belonging just to Mexicans.

Uranga urges us that we talk instead of insufficiency, which refers less to an individual or cultural neurosis, and more to an actual ontological relation before *an idea* (e.g., represented by the idea of European humanity), as well as to the ontological fact of being accidental. Uranga writes:

> Insufficiency, ontologically speaking, characterizes what is accident in relation to substance. *Every modality of being grounded on accident is partly grounded on an absence*, these modes of being are situated in an inconsistent and fractured base. (Uranga 2021, 103)

Insufficiency in relation to substance means one exists always in a state of *lack*, of deficiency, it is to exist as if one's very identity is formed—metaphysically, psychologically, and ontologically—on an incompletion, or, again, an absence. This is an original state, revealed to the Mexican person by historical fact: the trauma of conquest, the violence of colonialism, and the uncertainty and insecurity of independence have made insufficiency palpable. In this way, the being that constitutes Mexican being is a reduced being, a negative being, or a "minus" of being. Insufficient, or "[n]egatively conceived, the accident is a privation, an absence, a penury, a lack or defect of substance, an insufficient being" (Uranga 2021, 116).

Now, the fact that my "inferiority" shows up when I compare myself to others and find myself coming up short, or unable to measure up, points to this more profound insufficiency, or lack of being. Inferiority is an expression of that insufficiency. However, the profundity of insufficiency points to it being a more general condition of existence, one affecting both myself and the other with whom I compare myself. We are both insufficient and lack being in relation to the idea of perfection or substance.

Ultimately, the recognition of insufficiency is empowering. Mexicans arrive at the truth of being human and, in recognizing their insufficiency, are closer than their European counterparts to that truth because Mexicans know and *feel* their existence to be fragile, "always revocable," and always "threatened by displacement," that is, they know and *live* their existence as accidental. The truth, if we may speak of truths, is that accidentality and insufficiency are *all-there-is*. In short, insufficiency describes the mode of being of the human as an always already incomplete project—in existential terms, that she is a project of becoming.

2.3 *Nepantla*

We will not elaborate too much on nepantla here, as Chapter 2 is dedicated to this concept. Briefly, in the project of Mexistentialism, nepantla describes the in-betweeness of being—a being in-between being. *Not* a being in-between being and nonbeing, as this would simply signal existence as a being-toward-death. Rather, an in-betweenness that puts the human being in an uncomfortable middlehood that is neither ground nor void, but a space of convergence and divergence, of suspension and pendularity that neutralizes one's movements and puts us in, what seems like, a perpetual state of waiting and transition and on-the-wayness.

In this sense, then, our identity is a dis-identity, a dislocation, a being-there that is dynamic rather than static, one we can picture as a constant migration from coasts to valleys, from edges to centers, and peripheries to peripheries, without the possibility of settling in any one of them. Nepantla thus designates a middlehood that defines peoples whose (dis)identity is fluid, migratory, and undefined. Given its complexity and its role in defining *being Mexican*, or the being of

Mexican being, Uranga (2021) calls nepantla "the cardinal category of [a Mexican] ontology" (167).

2.4 *Zozobra*

While nepantla is a fundamental *ontological* category describing the nature of Mexican existence in general as in-betweeness, zozobra is an *ontic*, or existential, category describing the way in which the Mexican person actually experiences that being. (As with nepantla, I will not spend too much time on this concept here, and the reader is referred to Chapter 3.) Briefly, zozobra is the affective manifestation, or the feeling, that accompanies our being nepantla.

Zozobra names the anxiety of not knowing where one stands at any one time, it names the feeling of sinking and drowning that overtakes one in moments of despair or in times of catastrophe, and it names the feeling of being pulled to pieces by conflicting demands and expectations. In zozobra, one struggles to hold on to meaning or to find one's way given the available possibilities of existence. Uranga (2021) imagines it as a "mode of being that incessantly oscillates between two possibilities, between two affects, without knowing on which of these to depend, on which of these to cling to for justification" (180). I imagine it as the feeling of being quartered by uncertainties, as if by horses. This is zozobra, and Uranga thinks it manifests the nepantla nature of Mexican identity. As such, zozobra never gives us "a fixed and solid ground" [*punto fijo y roqueño*], but presents the world underfoot as "quicksand on which nothing firm can stand" (181). Luis Villoro (1949) adds that zozobra characterizes our being as accident, reflected in our constant pursuit of security, permanence, or substance. He writes: "The privileged sense of zozobra reveals the accidentality of being itself and of the world. This one appears as insubstantial and fragile; we thus try to flee from our own insubstantiality by seeking substance" (242).

Zozobra, as that calamitous feeling that all of our life's choices are dead-ends, that we are never secure in our choices, points back to that fundamental accidentality.

2.5 *Freedom*

Mexistentialism does not promote the notion of absolute freedom famously proposed in Sartre's *Being and Nothingness* (1992), as this does not seem to cohere with the "figure of the world" belonging to "post-Western," postcolonial national communities like Mexico. Certainly, a history of colonial subjugation and imperial intervention instilled in Mexican consciousness an unambiguous desire for freedom. However, the desired freedom is not absolute, but qualified, and takes the form of a "positive" freedom to commit or not commit oneself to (or be responsible for) one's liberation.

Hence, in his confrontation with Sartre, Leopoldo Zea attends not to the absolute freedom of Sartre's "early" existentialism, but to Sartre's "mature version" (e.g., *Critique of Dialectical Reason*), what Zea (2017) calls "situated, committed freedom" (135). It would be "irresponsible," according to Zea, to "maintain the idea of freedom in a full and absolute sense" when the whole of humanity is in crisis. What is needed, he says echoing the later Sartre, is a "[r]esponsible freedom, [one] aware of its limits . . . [one] always aware" (135). Zea thus endorses a view of freedom where the restriction imposed takes the form of commitment or responsibility. In this way, freedom and responsibility are two sides of the same coin; or as Zea puts it, "[w]here there is no responsibility, there is no freedom" (135).

On Luis Villoro's reading, absolute freedom is actually impossible because in my being free I find myself always already in a context of significance, one that "reveals the tightly woven fabric of phenomena that imprisons me" (147). The notion that there is a *prison of phenomena* in which I find myself refers to the fact that those things that stand around me (what Ortega calls the circumstance) mesmerize me, hold my attention, and thus limit or restrict my physical and psychical movements. This is an unavoidable imprisonment since one is always *in-the-world* and thus cannot *not* be involved in and with things. This might be seen as a *loss* of freedom, but for Villoro, it is the only kind of freedom we have.

True freedom is only possible in the encounter with the *other*, and it is a freedom only the other can attain. In appearing before me, the other reveals her freedom in her ability to "escape my conceptualizations" and, in revealing her freedom, I find that her freedom is made possible through me, or because of me, or in spite of me. More importantly, I become aware at that moment that I am willing to lose my freedom in the dialectic with the other as her "fate becomes mine" (149). As with Zea, freedom for Villoro is subordinated to responsibility: responsibility for another who escapes my grasp yet whose fate is tied to mine.

2.6 *Responsibility and Commitment*

Zea (2017) summarizes the Mexistentialist view of freedom: "our freedom is expressed in the form in which we assume the inevitable commitment to our circumstance" (126). This "inevitable commitment" is assumed because the fate of the "other"—the other person, the circumstance, the absolute—is "mine." What happens to my circumstances or to the other person happens to me, and vice versa. As Ortega (2000) put it in 1914, "if I do not save [my circumstance] I do not save myself" (45–6). I am thus responsibly committed to caring for that which is proximal to me and to my concerns. Zea (2017) explains:

> For what situation must we be responsible? What commitments must our philosophy responsibly make? After all, if we are to be faithful to [our philosophizing], we have to affirm that our *situation* is not that of Jean-Paul Sartre. Our situation is not that of the European bourgeoisie . . . Before making ourselves responsible for the world's commitments, we must be responsible for our own concrete situations. We must be conscious of our situation to make ourselves responsible for it. (137)

In this passage, we find the clue to the Mexistentialist difference. The "M" in Mexistentialism refers to the notion that "our situation is not that of Jean-Paul Sartre"—"our situation," that is, is *Mine*. Here, the "M" is tied to "Me." In fact, *my* situation is not that of either Jean-Paul Sartre or Zea. My situation is wholly mine, and I must be conscious of it and take responsibility for it before I make any commitments to abstract entities like "world" or "humanity." Of course, this does not mean that Mexistentialism advocates the type of narcissism that would prohibit caring for the world or for humanity, but that world and that humanity must be concrete and not abstract, it must be thought of as a *real* world and a *real* humanity in which I exist.

The task for Mexistentialism is ultimately to shepherd us to a recognition of our own responsibilities and commitments, which will be unique to us—as our circumstance, habitat, or world is unique to us. But this means facing accidentality, zozobra, nepantla, and the burden of *our particular* histories. This follows from Zea's (1949) claim that "existentialism does not wish to elude reality, does not evade it, it confronts it, assuming it with all of its consequences" (3).

2.7 *Humanism*

Accidentality, insufficiency, nepantla, and zozobra appear as defining characteristics of persons who live a "Mexican" existence, where "Mexican" is understood as *a* horizon of possible experience. But it is also a defining characteristic of human being as such, that is, of *what it means to be human.* Due mainly to the testimony of history, one that carries with it a familiarity with these existential and ontological realities, Mexicans are quick to identify them as *their* defining characteristics— even if pre-theoretically, in ordinary, non-philosophical, language. However, this does not mean that these define *only* Mexicans. For this reason, Uranga makes the rather suggestive proposal that genuine humanity is genuine only when it "resembles" that which is, in sense and experience, Mexican.

> It appears to us that considering the Mexican person in his being, or in his ontological aspect, serves or functions as a source for a sense of the human applicable to anything that pretends to represent itself as human. It is not about articulating lo mexicano (that which particularizes us) as human, but the opposite; it is about articulating the human in terms of lo mexicano. Lo mexicano is the point of

reference for the human; whatever resembles lo mexicano calibrates itself as human. (Uranga 2021, 109)

The call here is for an understanding of "the human" that reflects those things that which is Mexican that philosophically define it, namely, accident, insufficiency, zozobra, nepantla, and so on. But we must understand this in its proper light as this call is not, for instance, that the French or Canadians should suddenly seek to mimic Mexican being so as to be properly human. Such imitation would be inauthentic and an act of bad faith on their part. This call is for Mexicans themselves to recognize *their* own being as authentic and own up to it as Mexicans, to look nowhere else but to their own reality for that which is truly human, to accept it, and to live in accordance with that picture.

Elsewhere, in "Notes on an Ontology of Mexican Being," Uranga (1951) writes, "[a] call for the being of the Mexican does not serve any other purpose than to remind the Mexican person that in her style of life she has the norm [*pauta*] of the human, that if she puts on a mask she runs the risk of 'dehumanizing' herself" (126). In this, general sense, Mexistentialism demands that the standard of "humanity" we set for ourselves should not be abstract or foreign *to ourselves*, but reflective of our own concrete and familiar experience.

2.8 Death

In Mexistentialism, the relationship to death is one of coexistence and not one of possibility.

In *The Labyrinth of Solitude*, Octavio Paz (1985) writes: "there are two attitudes toward death: one, pointing forward, that conceives of it as creation; the other, pointing backward, that expresses itself as a fascination with nothingness or as a nostalgia for limbo" (61). Paz goes on to say that the attitude that points forward is found among the peoples of Europe and North America; the backward-pointing attitude is found in the peoples of Mexico. We may call the forward-pointing attitude, the instrumental attitude; the backward-pointing attitude may be referred to as the historical attitude (Sánchez 2013).

To say that one's attitude toward death is instrumental is to say that death, my death and death in general, is something that *is yet to happen*, it is an event of the future, always on the horizon and always a possibility. The historical attitude, on the other hand, is one which holds that death is a presence or a perpetual recovery of a past annihilation—a coexistence. The instrumental attitude is neatly described by Sigmund Freud (1950) when he says, "The goal of all life is death" (50). This means that life is a steady progress toward death. As a goal, or destination, death motivates life *forward*. Life's movement onward toward death is echoed by the cultural anthropologist Ernest Becker (1973) in *The Denial of Death*: "[T]he idea of death, the fear of it, haunts the human animal like nothing else; it is a mainspring of human activity—activity designed largely to avoid the fatality of death, to overcome it by denying in some way that it is the final destiny of man" (xvii). This instrumental view of death is the Western or North American attitude.

The second, historical, attitude is summarized by Uranga (2017) when he writes: "Death is the only thing that the Mexican does not leave for 'tomorrow'" (193). In other words, our being is not a "being-toward-death" but a "being-with-death," an experience in the now and not in the future. Mexicans coexist with death. Coexistence with death is much different than simply being aware of its inevitability. To coexist with death is to know it, to know it to be *there*; it is to live side by side with it and to share with it one's life; but it also means that, unlike the instrumental death that will eventually take everything away from me, historical death will take nothing away from me, since as an accomplished fact, there is nothing that I can give it. Uranga (2013) puts it this way:

> Death is not feared for the ends it brings nor because it impedes some mission, which doesn't exist, nor is it feared for ripping away a self that also does not exist. This is opposed to that extreme case, the German, which is Heidegger's, in which death is imagined as conferring upon life both individuality and totality. For the Spaniard and for the North American death takes away something, while for the German, it gives, but for the Mexican it neither gives nor takes because there's nothing to take and there's nothing to give. (194)

Ultimately, the omnipresence of death, its ordinariness and ubiquity, means that one does not long for it or fear it. Rather than a longing, Mexistentialism highlights a nostalgia, a kind of presence in memory. This is because death has already happened yet remains, intermingling with the present as ghosts or spirits; it is with us as a persistent memory, as a presence that neither gives nor takes away but remains a coexistence.

2.9 *Culture*

Culture is a broad interpretive framework; culture is that *through* which one relates oneself to the rest of the world. Culture can be a "figure of the world." In the feminist Mexistentialism of Rosario Castellanos (1925–74), for instance, culture is the circumstance. However, this is not a circumstance that must be "saved," as Ortega implores, but one that must be challenged and overcome.

We are thrown into a culture not of our own making. That's an existential fact. But this culture into which we have been thrown, according to Castellanos (2017), "has been created almost exclusively by men" (206). What this means for Castellanos is that what a woman *is* or *could be* will be decided by an interpretive framework created by men. A woman's possibilities of existence—her identity, attributes, behaviors, and roles—are determined in advance by that patriarchal framework. As such, she is always already "subjugated to outdated atavisms" (Hierro 1981, 29). Ultimately, transcending this framework is presented as an existential project that women (and, ultimately, all peripheral peoples) must take on.

This notion of transcending determining frameworks (whether these are remnants of colonialism or other influences) is key to Mexistentialism, especially given the oppressive authority and persistence of colonial power in Mexican history and the necessity to move beyond it. We find the need to transcend this power in Villoro, Zea, and Uranga, but it is made a central motif in existential project of Castellanos. In, what I'm calling, Castellano's feminist Mexistentialism, transcendence becomes a real task for women by the fact that they are doubly oppressed in *Mexican* society: once by being *women* and again by being *Mexican* women.

In making her case, Castellanos (2017) insists that Mexican culture is both a remnant of colonial power and patriarchal. According to Castellanos, the way to escape culture, as she understands it, is by confronting cultural categories. This challenge requires that each woman fully affirm herself as what she is while denying what she is told she is; this challenge requires the "transcendence" of that "myth" constructed by man.

According to Castellanos, such transcendence is possible in the act of writing. Writing is a means for woman "to set her limits, to affirm herself solidly within her individuality, to give herself her own echo" (214). In giving herself her own echo, she invents herself: "It isn't even enough to discover who we are. We have to invent ourselves" (cited in German 2018). This process of invention drowns out the culture's echo, allowing her to "transcend" cultural and inherited expectations. "Finding themselves in need of letting themselves go, of transcendence, they encounter another channel, the literary, and it does not matter if it is adequate or not, so long as it is possible" (Castellanos 2017, 214).

Castellanos' Mexistentialism means to orient women to the value of their own subjectivity. Delving into themselves in the act of writing can be seen by the male culture as a denial of obligations or traditional community, but Castellanos (2017) implores women to affirm their "narcissism . . . uncompromising subjectivity . . . fierce individuality" (215). This valuing of subjectivity—which is an "essential" trait of Mexistentialism and Mexican philosophy generally—is also a rejection of a Western philosophical value, of what Zea calls "the imperial passion" (see Sánchez 2016), namely, the Eurocentric obsession with disinterestedness, abstractness, and objectivity. Castellanos (2017) thinks that Mexican women are existentially positioned to challenge the imperial passion by taking advantage of their subjectivity. The imploration is to

[dive] deeper each time into their own being, rather than making unfortunate, failed attempts to evade themselves, attempts that do not

take her as far as she wants to be, but far enough so as to place her on false ground that she neither knows nor can control. What we can hope for, however, is that she inverts the direction of that movement . . . turning it toward her own being, and with such force that it may be able to overcome those immediate and fragile peripheries, and allow her to dive into those depths where she might reach her true and, until now, inviolable roots, pushing aside those conventional images of femininity that men have prepared for her, and thus she may form her own image, an image based on her personal, irreplaceable experience, an image that may nor may not coincide with that other image. (215)

In this way, Castellanos proposes an existential project of overcoming: overcoming culture, overcoming history, and overcoming the self. With this, we can say that the project of feminist Mexistentialism has to do with gaining a clear recognition of one's place in the world (i.e., Mexican culture), of one's self, and, simultaneously, of those "fragile peripheries" that construct cultural, historical, identity. The end result of these efforts should be the transcendence of those "conventional imagines of femininity that men have prepared for her," leading to both self-affirmation and freedom. Graciela Hierro (1981) sums up Castellanos' philosophical project: it is all about setting up the conditions for the possibility of "being a Mexican woman and a free human being" (29).

3. In Place of a Conclusion: *Can I Be a Mexistentialist?*

Mexican philosophers approach existentialism not as a philosophical fad, a charge that some have leveled against postwar French existentialism, or even as a rigorous philosophical method, but as the possibility of a critical philosophical articulation of their own situated reality, implying also the possibility for a more responsible engagement with the history, culture, and the future of that reality. Mexistentialism, understood in this context, allows the articulation of a mode of existence belonging to historically marginal and peripheral peoples, those who have been deemed "accidental" to the global designs of colonial power.

In this chapter, I have tried to offer a profile of what I call "Mexistentialism." Not only does Mexistentialism mark the emergence of a philosophical program preoccupied by cultural and historical identity and authenticity, but insofar as it insists on the relevance of cultural or national identity in philosophy, it presents a challenge to the hegemonic feel of Western philosophy.

While European existentialism paints a picture of radical individuality as thrown, absolutely free, mired in anxiety, and projected always toward an unknown *to come*, Mexistentialism conceives of the human person as always already engaged in circumstantial realities. For Mexistentialists such as Villoro, Zea, Castellanos, and Uranga, to exist is to commune, to care, and to engage. Accidentality and insufficiency, nepantla and zozobra, while characteristic of our mode of being, do not exempt us from our responsibility to others. On the contrary, insufficiency and accidentality, by pointing to the fragility and finitude of human existence, call on us to live fuller, more caring, and more generous lives. In other words, consciousness of our insufficiency and accidentality calls on us to take responsibility for the other by articulating, on her behalf, the urgency to pursue a genuine and authentic existence and the necessity to forgo the impossible assimilation to purity and perfection. This is a moral orientation we find in feminist Mexistentialism as well as in Mexistentialism generally. In other words, the move that follows a deep dive into our own being (as in Castellanos) is a move outward. Villoro (2017) explains, one must "get out of insular consciousness so as to arrive at community consciousness" because "community is the form of life which is superior . . . and [consists only] in a personal life praxis which is interpersonal and ethically motivated" (309).

My hope is that we may come to talk about Mexistentialism alongside French and German existentialism or, even, "American existentialism" (see Cotkin 2005). Mexistentialism, like its French or German varieties, is rooted in the notion that human existence is a never-ending project of precarious and uncertain becoming and overcoming.

The existentialist urge in Mexico emerges from the suspicion that the Western philosophical inheritance is biased and, even, arrogant;

from the suspicion that philosophical universality and generality are historical constructs serving the interests of European colonial power. This is why Uranga (2021) complains that "we are not certain of the existence of man in general . . . [or of] what passes itself off as man in general, namely, generalized European humanity" (107). The movement away from this doubtful "man in general" requires a return to origins, that is, to the *lived world* of the non-European, where the generalizations of Western, Eurocentric philosophy may not always fit.

After all is said and done, the real, practical question, becomes: can I, or you, be a Mexistentialist? If my picture of the world involves the notion that my existence is accidental and that no existence is substantial or absolutely self-sufficient; that my being is a being in nepantla, or always in-between and always in transition; that I experience my nepantla in zozobra as a struggle to hold on to conflicting demands placed on my person; that my freedom is qualified and that my freest action would be to commit myself to the needs of my immediate circumstance; but also, that I am determined by culture only to the extent that I allow it; and, finally, if my picture of the world includes the view that death is not something to look forward to (or fear), but an accomplished fact, an event with which I coexist, then, yes, I (and you), can be Mexistentialists. As a Mexistentialist, moreover, one does not behave carelessly or distant toward oneself or one's world, as, for instance, the protagonist of Camus' *The Stranger*; on the contrary, one's behavior is caring and involved, a manifestation of understanding life's instability and finitude.

*   *   *

Mexistentialism is but one way to talk about what makes individual existence unique, genuine, and worth a philosophical articulation. But in insisting on the "M" without parentheses, we affirm it as a different and necessary way, as a way to decentralize and decenter philosophy itself as a global project of life. Most importantly, it affirms for us all, Mexican, Latinx, and other peoples historically relegated to peripheries and margins of philosophy, that we are, and are *as a matter of fact,* or genuinely, or authentically, always already grappling with human existence. We thus echo and paraphrase Portilla's proud admission that some of us "are existentialists from birth" (Portilla 2017).

I invoke Mexistentialism here as a concept that captures a reading of existence through a situated, post-Western perspective.

Questions for Discussion

Introduction

1. How does a historical difference translate into a philosophical difference according to the Introduction?
2. Why is it important to insist on Mexican philosophy's inclusion into "world philosophies"?
3. How does the author arrive at the suggestion that Mexican philosophy is "post-Western"?
4. Are the "reasons" given by the author as to why Mexican philosophy is not yet normalized convincing?
5. Do you agree that there is a difference between Mexican philosophy and *filosofía Mexicana*?
6. According to the author, it is necessary to diversify our syllabus. Do you think Mexican philosophy contributes significantly to that diversification?

Chapter 1: Relajo

1. Relajo is a "suspension of seriousness." What is seriousness? Discuss the ways in which values and seriousness are related. How is it that to suspend seriousness implies the suspension of values?
2. Consider a social, cultural, or political institution. What does it mean to say that it is held together by values? Discuss.
3. Relajo individuals, that is, relajientos, pose a particular risk to a well-ordered society. What are these risks? Why is a relajiento not enough to bring about relajo?

4. Why is the "apretado" the opposite of the relajiento? Describe these two types of personalities as they may appear in contemporary society.
5. According to the author, while it can be argued that relajo can be thought to be a decolonial, liberatory strategy, it is not. Summarize the argument.
6. How is relajo a threat to a well-ordered society? Discuss.

Chapter 2: Nepantla

1. Discuss the different characterizations of nepantla outlined at the beginning of the chapter. Which one is more familiar to your own experience?
2. Discuss the ways in which nepantla defines *your* own existential or ontological situation.
3. I say that nepantla is ontological—what does this mean?
4. It could be argued that there is a problem in referring to that nepantla is simply "the middle" or the "in between." Why would this be problematic?
5. As a "being in between," to be nepantla is to be unsettled. From a purely existential perspective, human beings are all unsettled; can we then say that nepantla describes all human beings? What's at stake in making this claim? Who would be left out of such an account, if anyone?
6. According to the author, there is a difference between zozobra and nepantla. Without looking ahead, what could this difference be?

Chapter 3: Zozobra

1. What is zozobra? How is it different than mere existential anxiety?
2. In what ways is zozobra descriptive of Mexican being, according to the authors discussed?

3. If there is an upside to zozobra, can you identify it? Otherwise, is zozobra strictly a negative phenomenon?
4. According to Uranga, how does zozobra set up the conditions for the possibility of community?
5. Looking back at Chapter 2, what, according to the author, is the difference between nepantla and zozobra?
6. Discuss three ways in which zozobra shows up in our contemporary world?

Chapter 4: Corazonadas

1. What epistemological problem does Uranga's notion of corazonda seek to solve? Does it succeed? Why or why not?
2. Consider Pascal's notion that "the heart has its reasons that reason does not know." Discuss the ways in which Uranga's notion of corazonada resembles Pascal's description of knowing with the heart.
3. Identify some "truths" that can be grasped by corazonadas.
4. How is a corazonada different and similar to intuition? Why did Uranga think that intuition was "confused"?
5. How is a corazonada different and similar to gut feelings?
6. In what ways can corazonada help *explain* certain aspects of our current post-truth age? Give examples.

Chapter 5: Tik

1. Discuss the different conceptions of community mentioned by Portilla? Why do they fall short?
2. What is the main difference between Portilla's description of genuine community and the Tojolab'al notion of "tik"?
3. Is the sort of inclusive community, or radical we-ness, discussed in this chapter possible? Why or why not?

4. Consider the concept of democracy. Is democracy compatible with the Tojolab'al notion of community?
5. What happens to the individual in a "tik" situation?

Chapter 6: The Figure of the World

1. What is the "domination thesis"?
2. What is a "figure of the world"? What is a "colonial" figure of the world?
3. Discuss the three stages in the understanding of the other that Villoro outlines.
4. How is Villoro's "figure of the world" related to the notion of interpretive frameworks as understood in the history of philosophy?
5. What did Sahagún achieve that other colonizers could not? How is that a lesson for us today?
6. According to Villoroi, what is one way to overcome an arrogant interpretive framework?

Chapter 7: Mexistentialism

1. Why does the author "remove the parenthesis" from (M) existentialism? And why does the author claim this to be significant? Do you think it matters?
2. In your own words, describe the value of existentialism according to Mexican philosophers.
3. What is "accidentality" and why is it an important Mexistentialist concept?
4. Is there a clear difference between Mexistentialism and European existentialism? If there is no clear difference, why do you think

that the author insists that there is? As you consider this question, think about this: Why would it be important to distinguish between African existentialism and French existentialism?

5. Can you be a Mexistentialist? If not, why not? If so, how so?

Further Reading

In English

Anzaldúa, Gloria. 2012. *Borderlands/La Frontera*. San Francisco: Aunt Lute Books.
   Problematizes the notion of Chicanix identity by deploying the concept of "nepantla" beautifully and effectively. One of the first incursions into the history of Mexican philosophy *for the sake* of non-Mexican life.

Bartra, Roger. 1992. *The Cage of Melancholy: Identity and Metamorphosis in the Mexican Character*, translated by Christopher J. Hill. New Brunswick: Rutgers University Press.
   A major work in late twentieth-century Mexican intellectual history. In it, Bartra rigorously critiques what he calls the *ideology* of "lo mexicano," which, he argues, was promoted by the intellectuals of the Mexican ruling class for the purposes of maintaining the Mexican status quo. Bartra specifically criticizes the work of *el Hiperión* (and, particularly, Uranga) as a nationalistic mechanism of colonial oppression constructed to reproduce myth; it was not what *los hiperiónes* claimed, namely, a rational reconstruction of a real way of life.

De la Cruz, Sor Juana Inés. 2006. *Selected Works*, translated by Edith Grossman. New York: W.W. Norton.
   The writings of the fifteenth-century nun Sor Juana Inés de la Cruz signal the arrival of critical feminist philosophy to the New World.

Durán, Diego. 1994. *History of the Indies of New Spain*, translated by Doris Heyden. Norman: University of Oklahoma Press, 1994.
   A monumental tome in the history of the Conquest of Mexico. It is here that Durán recounts his encounters with peoples that existed *neither* according to a European nor an indigenous religion/ontology but in between, in *nepantla*.

Hurtado, Guillermo and Robert Eli Sanchez. 2020. "Philosophy in Mexico," in *The Stanford Encyclopedia of Philosophy*, edited by Edward N. Zalta,

Downloaded, March 14, 2022, https://plato.stanford.edu/archives/win2020/entries/philosophy-mexico/.
Expansive entry on Mexican philosophy which recounts the history (from pre-Hispanic times to the present), figures, major themes, and the current state of the tradition in Mexico and the United States. This should be the first stop for anyone seeking an authoritative introduction into Mexican philosophy.

León-Portilla, Miguel. 1967. *Aztec Thought and Culture: A Study of the Ancient Nahuatl Mind.* Norman: University of Oklahoma Press.
The first authoritative text on the philosophy of the ancient Nahuatl. Of significance is León-Portilla's recalibration of the Eurocentric notion of philosophy, offering one that is inclusive of other knowledges and other ways of life, specifically, Aztec thought and metaphysics.

Maffie, James. 2015. *Aztec Philosophy: Understanding a World in Motion.* Boulder: University of Colorado Press.
Maffie settles the debate regarding the existence and nature of an Aztec "philosophy" with a profound and scholarly account and analysis of Aztec metaphysics. His discussions of napantla are of particular interest as they will help the reader better situate and understand Uranga's use of this important term.

Oliver, Amy. 2022. "Valuing Mexican Philosophy: Suspect Behavior or Life Affirming Path?" *Journal of Mexican Philosophy* 1, no. 1: 1–12.
This essay juxtaposes Mexican philosophy with world philosophies and philosophy writ large, and offers an assessment of salient moments in the history of Mexican philosophy (including indigenous contributions, Sor Juana, anti-positivist thinkers, and innovative philosophical concepts/terms) and suggests their applicability to non-Mexican circumstances.

Ortega y Gasset, José. 2000. *Meditations on Quixote*, translated by Evelyn Rugg and Diego Marín. Chicago: University of Illinois Press.
Published in 1914, the significance of this text to Latin American philosophy cannot be overstated. It is here that Ortega introduces the circumstantialist principle "I am myself and my circumstances." With this principle in hand, Mexican philosophers found justification for their situated philosophizing and motivation to construct "la filosofía de lo mexicano."

Paz, Octavio. 1985. *The Labyrinth of Solitude*. New York: Grove Press Inc.
Paz's famous study of the Mexican character, first published in 1951. Highly influenced by contemporary discussions on Mexicanness, Paz seeks to lend his study a sociological base. Emilio Uranga dedicates his *Analysis* to Paz in an effort to philosophically mirror it and, perhaps, overcome it.

Ramos, Samuel. 1962. *Profile of Man and Culture in Mexico*, translated by Peter G. Earle. McAllen: Texas Pan-American Press.
Perhaps the most important work in twentieth-century Mexican philosophy, Ramos' *Profile* proposes "inferiority" as the defining characteristic of the Mexican character. Historically informing this Alderean psychoanalytic concept, the *Profile* continues to arouse discussion. It is to the *Profile*'s main arguments against which Uranga reacts in his *Analysis*.

Romanell, Patrick. 1952. *Making of the Mexican Mind: A Study in Recent Mexican Thought*. Lincoln: University of Nebraska Press.
The first authoritative history of Mexican philosophy in English. It paints a picture of an autochthonous movement of philosophy up until the year of publication—1952. Although it says very little about the Hiperión group, the narrative it presents beautifully sets up the event of Hiperión.

Sánchez, Carlos Alberto. 2008. "Heidegger in Mexico: On Emilio Uranga's Ontological Hermeneutics." *Continental Philosophy Review* 41: 441–61.
An introductory foray into Emilio Uranga's Heideggerian influences in English. The paper seeks to position Uranga's appropriation as faithful to the existential hermeneutic while also going beyond it.

Sánchez, Carlos Alberto. 2012. *The Suspension of Seriousness: On the Phenomenology of Jorge Portilla*. Albany: SUNY Press.
An introduction and analysis to Jorge Portilla's *Fenomenología del relajo* (1963), published with a translation. A critical reading of Jorge Portilla's famous text. It situates Portilla as a philosopher of values and culture. It also introduces *el grupo Hiperión* as an important philosophical group to an English-speaking philosophical audience for the first time.

Sánchez, Carlos Alberto. 2016. *Contingency and Commitment: Mexican Existentialism and the Place of Philosophy*. Albany: SUNY Press.

A critical appraisal of mid-twentieth-century Mexican existentialism, specifically "la filosofía de lo mexicano" of *el grupo Hiperión* (Jorge Portilla, Leopoldo Zea, Luis Villoro, and Emilio Uranga). The principal claim here is that Mexican existentialism in particular and Mexican philosophy in general lend privilege to place and circumstance at the expense of abstract universalism.

Sánchez, Carlos Alberto and Robert Eli Sanchez (eds.). 2017. *Mexican Philosophy in the 20th Century: Essential Readings*. New York: Oxford University Press.

The first comprehensive anthology of twentieth-century Mexican philosophy in translation. The anthology contains articles on Mexican philosophy from 1910 to 1960.

Sánchez, Carlos Alberto. 2018. "The Gift of Mexican Historicism." *Continental Philosophical Review* 51, no. 3: 438–57.

This paper focuses on Emilio Uranga's historicism. It argues for the significance and value of historicism for philosophy, but especially for the philosophizing of marginalized groups.

Sánchez, Carlos Alberto and Francisco Gallegos. 2020. *The Disintegration of Community: On the Social and Political Philosophy of Jorge Portilla*. Albany: SUNY Press.

This volume includes previously untranslated minor essays of Portilla together with six critical reflections by the authors. While the focus is on a political reading of Portilla's "other essays," the critical reflections also touch upon Portilla's phenomenology and social philosophy.

Sanchez, Robert Eli (ed). 2020. *Latin American and Latinx Philosophy: A Collaborative Introduction*. New York: Routledge.

A collection of essays on Latin American and Latinx philosophy which includes a number of essays on Mexican philosophy of culture. It is a great resource for those wanting to situate themselves in the contemporary debates surrounding this tradition and its various offshoots.

Uranga, Emilio. 2018. "The Philosophy of Mexicanness," translation and introduction by Carlos Alberto Sánchez and Robert Eli Sanchez. *Aeon*. https://aeon.co/classics/to-be-accidental-is-to-be-human-on-the-philosophy-of-mexicanness.

This publication includes an annotated version of Uranga's "Essay on the Ontology of the Mexican," as well as an introduction to that essay by Sánchez and Sanchez.

Vargas, Manuel. 2019. "The Philosophy of Accidentality." *Journal of the American Philosophical Association* 6, issue 4: 391–409.

Vargas appeals to Uranga's notion of accidentality to offer his own interpretation of the concept, one that is richer and capable of broader applications. Vargas' analytical rigor makes sense of Uranga's philosophy for a new Anglo-American audience.

Vargas, Manuel. 2022. "If Aristotle Had Cooked: The Philosophy of Sor Juana." *Journal of Mexican Philosophy* 1, no. 1: 13–38.

Reflecting on the philosophy of this highly influential in the history of Mexican philosophy, what he calls, social fallibilism into her work, that is, the view that what we can know and do are dependent on somewhat fragile features of both agents and their social and material contexts. It is a prescient picture of human agency, where central features of it—including freedom and knowledge—are always relational in their realization and chronically vulnerable to defeat.

Vasconcelos, José. 2022. "The New Law of Three Stages," translated by Clinton Tolley. *Journal of Mexican Philosophy* 1, no. 1: 54–63.

Writing against the prevailing positivism in Mexico, Vasconcelos offers a reimagining of Comte's philosophy.

Zea, Leopoldo. 2004. *Positivism in Mexico*, translated by Josephine H. Schulte. Austin: University of Texas Press.

Zea's first book takes a critical look at Mexican positivism. First published in 1943, it is Zea's critical introduction to the positivistic ideology that dominated Mexico during the second half of the nineteenth century. Adopted as the state ideology, it sought to maintain colonial forms of exploitation under the guise of a national "order of progress." A deeply influential book in the history of Mexican ideas.

In Spanish (Selected)

Barreda, Gabino. 1901. "Oracion Civica Pronunciada en Guanajuato el 16 de septiembre del ano de 1867." *Revista Positiva*, no. 9: 381–405.

A public oration given in 1867 by Mexico's premier nineteenth-century philosopher on the virtues of self-reliance in culture, economics, and philosophy.

Cuéllar Moreno, José Manuel. *La revolución inconclusa: La filosofía de Emilio Uranga, artífice oculto del PRI*. México: Ariel, 2018.
An important examination of Emilio Uranga's political involvement and the manner in which his political activities were influenced (or not influenced) by his philosophical views. It argues against the notion that Uranga was an ideologue of the Mexican government during and after the events of 1968.

Gaos, José. "Epistolario y Papeles Privados," in en *Obras Completas XIX*, edited by Alfonso Rangel Guerra. México: Universidad Nacional Autónoma de México, 1999.
Indispensable for anyone interested in mid-twentieth-century Mexican philosophy. Gaos, through his lectures and translations, motivated Mexican existentialism and the philosophy of Mexicanness. In these "personal papers" we are invited to directly witness his involvement in the life and times of Mexican philosophy. His influence on Uranga and his impact on Mexican philosophy are clarified in journal entries and letters to friends and others.

Guerra, Ricardo. "Una historia del Hiperión." *Los Universitarios*, no. 18: 1984.
A first-hand autobiographical account that discusses the actual activities and internal politics of the group. Guerra was one of its founding members.

Hurtado, Guillermo (ed.). *El Hiperión*. México: Universidad Nacional Autónoma de México, 2006. The first anthology of key texts from *el grupo Hiperión*.
The "Introduction" by Hurtado gives a panoramic view of Hiperión's origins, activities, and legacy. It is an indispensable text for anyone interested in the overall significance of this important philosophical group.

Hurtado, Guillermo. 2008. *El búho y la serpiente*. México: Coordinacion de Humanidades.
A collection of essays on contemporary Mexican philosophy by Mexico's premier authority on its history. In a key and often cited essay, Hurtado distinguishes between two models of philosophy: the model of modernization and the model of authenticity, arguing that twentieth-century philosophy falls into one of these two modes. In general, the collection highlights the problematics of taking Mexico as a theme in philosophical investigation, offering both a critique and an invitation for those who would choose to do so.

Hurtado, Guillermo. 2022. "Notas para una crítica filosófica del malinchismo." *Journal of Mexican Philosophy* 1, no. 1: 39–53.

This paper seeks to overcome psychologistic or ontologistic interpretations of the philosophy of lo mexicano in order to lend it political trajectory. It examines and criticizes the phenomenon of malinchismo, understood as an enduring mechanism of domination in terms of both external colonialism and internal colonialism, and an indispensable project for a version of Mexican philosophy that aims to transform our national reality.

Pereda, Carlos. 2013. *La filosofia en Mexico en el siglo XX: Apuntes de un participante*. Mexico: Direccion General de Publicaciones.

Pereda weaves autobiographical detail with philosophical analysis and critique in this memoir of twentieth-century Mexican philosophy. He recounts his encounters and associations with Mexico's most significant thinkers.

Santos Ruiz, Ana. 2015. *Los hijos de los dioses: El Grupo filosófico Hiperión y la filosofía de lo mexicano*. México: Bonilla Artigas Editores.

This is a highly researched and immensely informative commentary on the political significance of the philosophy of Mexicanness. It makes several controversial claims about Uranga's role in the 1968 student massacre of Tlateloco, namely, suggesting Uranga's complicity as an ideologue of the Mexican state.

Troncoso Pérez, Ramón. 2011. "Nepantla, una aproximación al término," in *Tierras prometidas. De la colonia a la independencia*, edited by Bernat Castany, et al., 375–98. Barcelona: Centro para la Edición de los Clásicos Españoles-UAB.

Troncoso Pérez delves deep into the textual origins of "nepantla." Looking at Spanish chronicles of the Conquest of New Spain, Troncoso's analysis helps us understand the evolution and appropriation of this important philosophical concept, one to which Uranga gave special ontological privilege.

Uranga, Emilio. 1948. "Merleau-Ponty: fenomenología y existencialismo." *Filosofía y Letras* 15, no. 30: 235–50.

Uranga's introductory analysis of Merleau-Ponty's existential phenomenology. In it, Uranga aims to paint Merleau-Ponty as a philosopher of the circumstance, validating in this way his own long-term scholarly project.

Uranga, Emilio. 1949. "Dos teorias de la muerte: Sartre y Heidegger." *Filosofía y Letras* 27, no. 33: 55–71.

As well as discussing Sartre's and Heidegger's views on death, Uranga sheds light on the Mexican idea of death, which he contrasts with the "Western" or European idea of death.

Uranga, Emilio. 1949. "Dialogo con Maurice Merleau-Ponty." *Mexico en la cultura*, March 13, 1949.

This article reports a conversation with Merleau-Ponty that took place early in the spring of 1949 in Mexico City. On the invitation of *los Hiperiónes*, Merleau-Ponty visited Mexico City and gave a series of lectures on existentialism and phenomenology, much to the delight and enthusiasm of the young existential upstarts.

Uranga, Emilio. 1951. "Notas para un estudio del mexicano." *Cuadernos Americanos*, 10, no. 3: 114–128.

Uranga's "notes" for a method suitable for the study of Mexican being. It is a prelude to the work that will come about in *Analysis*, focusing on the existential-phenomenological approach required for such a task.

Uranga, Emilio. 2013. *Análisis del ser del mexicano y otros escritos sobre la filosofía de lo mexicano (1949-1952)*, edited by Guillermo Hurtado. México: Bonilla Artigas Editores.

This is the latest edition of Uranga's *Análisis*. It comes with a larger selection of minor works, journalistic pieces, and letters.

Villegas, Abelardo. 1979. *La filosofía de lo mexicano*. México: Universidad Nacional Autónoma de México. The definitive guide to the "philosophy of Mexicanness."

A comprehensive analysis of "Mexican" philosophy beginning in the twentieth century. More than a historical overview, it is also critical. It finds and highlights the philosophical pitfalls with the movement and with the philosophical results.

Villoro, Luis. 1990. "Emilio Uranga: La accidentalidad como fundamento de la cultura Mexicana," in Emilio Uranga, *Analysis del ser del mexicano*. Guanajuato: Gobierno del Estado de Guanajuato.

An indispensable introduction to *Analysis* by one of Uranga's most celebrated contemporaries and one of Mexico's most important philosophers.

This essay is included in the 1990 edition of Uranga's *Analysis*; it historically and thematically contextualizes the work around the concept of "accidentality." Villoro's analyses are original and valuable.

Wimer, Javier. 2005. "La muerte de un filsofó." *Revista de la Universidad de Mexico*, no. 17: 27–33.
Written almost two decades after Uranga's death, this article vibrantly portrays Uranga's last days, connecting the fall of the great philosopher to key moments in his philosophical life.

Zirión Quijano, Antonio. 2003. *Historia de la fenomenología en México.* Morelia: jitanjáfora Morelia Editorial.
A detailed history of phenomenology in Mexico, starting with early adopters of the Husserlian method, taking the reader through the height of phenomenological activity in Mexico during the 1940s and 1950s, and into contemporary times. Zirión Quijano's emphasis is on phenomenological work, rather than existential or analytic, and so it is a great resource for students of this tradition.

Notes

Introduction

1 The idea is that legitimizing a philosophical tradition will depend on whether or not it is written about in English. According to the Mexican philosopher, Guillermo Hurtado, Mexican philosophy is in the process of such legitimization (2021).

2 I will address what I mean by "outside of Mexico," see Section 5.

3 On what is meant by "world philosophies," see Kirloskar-Steinbach and Kalmanson (2021).

4 The common tendency (read: colonial tendency) is to group Mexican philosophy with Peruvian philosophy, as well as other South American philosophical traditions, into the umbrella category "Latin American philosophy." This, of course, erases the intra-traditional differences and, in fact, conceals all evidence that particular peoples deeply cared about what it is they, themselves and for their own reasons, called "philosophy" as well as the reasons why they engaged in such activities in the first place. An example of this can be found in Brian W. Van Norden's bibliography of, what he calls, "Less Commonly Taught Philosophies." While under Chinese, Indian, and Jewish traditions Van Norden includes both general studies as well as individual philosophical treatise that exemplify the richness of that particular tradition, the entry for Latin American philosophy includes, almost exclusively, only general studies that introduce readers to Latin American philosophy as a whole. On this reading, there is only one homogenous Latin American philosophical tradition—there are no differences, then, between the Argentinian philosophical tradition and the Peruvian philosophical tradition (this is false). While this is only one example, I think it typifies and reflects the current state of the academy somewhat accurately. On this reading, the Mexican philosophical tradition simply does not exist (see Van Norden 2022).

5 On the persistent force of these "ideological currents," see Kirloskar-Steinbach and Kalmanson (2021).

6 We've previously argued that Mexican philosophy is a product of twentieth century, with origins in the Mexican Revolution and its aftermaths (Sánchez and Sanchez 2017, "Introduction").

7 Thus, Uranga (1951) says, of the double origins of the Mexican character: "[t]he indigenous is a foundation of our character, a matrix; the Spanish, on the other hand, is a variation, a point of/for resistance" (127).

8 I have previously abbreviated this as "circumstantialism" and "auscultatory analysis" (See, Sánchez 2016). Elsewhere, we defined Mexican philosophy as being "(1) self-reflective . . . (2) critical; and (3) affirmative or positive" by which we meant that it reflected a critical concern with a burdensome colonial inheritance (Sánchez and Sanchez 2017, xxx).

9 This is a definition Hurtado also finds restrictive and outdated.

10 What I call "circumstantialism" was first proposed by José Ortega y Gasset *Meditations on Quixote* of 1914,where he states: "I am myself and my circumstance; and, if I cannot save it, I cannot save myself" (45). Zea is clearly indebted to Ortega, especially in the former's adoption and appropriation of this thesis.

11 The late Jorge J. E. Gracia more clearly articulated this historical breakdown: "the first—*rebellion*—is characterized by the backlash against positivism and the subsequent development of foundations for future philosophical movements (ca.1910–1940). The second—*normalcy*—is characterized by the achievement of a degree of institutionalization and normalization in the philosophical profession (1940–1960). The third period—*maturity* (ca. 1960 to the present)—is distinguished by the degree of professional and philosophical maturity attained by Latin American philosophers" (Gracia 2018).

12 William Cooper (2010) explains this further: "a more careful and methodological study of works in philosophy published in Europe and to some degree in the United States. In some cases, what resulted from this more thorough study was critical exposition and analysis of the texts being studied. With some thinkers this study became the basis for the development of a philosophical perspective with a quality of its own. During this period of 'normal' development, the study of philosophy becomes more widespread and the number of persons devoted to philosophical work increases considerably. Furthermore, as one would expect, the variety in philosophical perspectives also multiplies the quality of the thought it takes on added strength" (129).

13 This period lasts less than two decades (mid-1940s until late 1960s), and is highlighted by the Hiperion group, the editorial book series *Mexico y lo Mexicano*, and, in the end, by its rejection by writers like Jose Revueltas, Rosario Castellanos, and Abelardo Villegas.

14 This is a term from Abelardo Villegas. About this Villegas (1992) writes: "In Europe there were not only great philosophers but also those who recognized them, who valued them, and who made an adequate echo for them. With Mexican philosophers, however, there was a kind of cannibalism: they devoured each other in the worst cases, their works fell into a conspiracy of silence, as if no one had written anything!" (39).

15 Luise Antony (2016) writes: "Our knowledge institutions, as they are currently constituted, neglect to a criminal degree the needs and interests of socially subordinated people. Indeed, these institutions are increasingly oriented toward the interests of the wealthiest and most powerful people in our society—a trend that is vastly accelerated by the erosion of public funding for education and research. The demographic homogeneity of the academy and the laboratory certainly reflects the racism, sexism, and economic subordination that silences voices and limits opportunities" (171).

16 This is not to say that Mexican philosophy has not sought this arrogant sort of universality. The history of Mexican philosophy is a history of grappling with what philosophy is supposed to be. We could describe this struggle as one between universality and particularity. It involves both the resistance to and the desire to conform to the Standard Dogma of Philosophy. This struggle, however, has placed Mexican philosophy in a double bind, one in which Mexican philosophers find themselves trapped in a *desire* for universality so as to seem properly "philosophical" while knowing that particularity is the only way to assure that they're speaking from and about Mexico—that they're lending voice to their own social, cultural, and historical experience. The double bind is a problem for Mexican philosophy, as it must now consider that either universality or particularity will have to be sacrificed at the altar authenticity: it risks being authentically philosophical if it insists on its particularity but it risks genuineness if it folds to the demands of the Standard Dogma. Thus, the double bind gives rise to metaphilosophical questions related to philosophical originality, in both senses of the term (as novelty or origin), and to the nature of the philosophical as such, namely, questions about

its boundaries or limits. But, this is already *doing* Mexican philosophy, as the tendency is not to favor universality or particularity, but to preserve enough from both so as to resist totalization while ensuring that some sort of difference is maintained. One must tread the horns of the double bind and fall somewhere in the middle.

17 Hurtado originally gave these comments in response to my book *Emilio Uranga's Analysis of Mexican Being* at a conference celebrating Emilio Uranga's birthday. "II Coloquio internacional sobre Emilio Uranga y el Grupo Hiperion," August 25–27, 2021. Mexico City, Instituto de Investigaciones Filosoficas. Video of the panel can be accessed here: https://youtu.be/xxjiRtjt71o

Chapter 1

1 I've written about the difficulties of translating this concept. See Sánchez (2012).

2 Translated and included as an Appendix to the aforementioned work, *The Suspension of Seriousness* (Sánchez 2012).

3 Manfred Frings (1997) attributes a "functional" theory of value to Max Scheler, who considers values as existing, not *a priori*, but only *with* or *among* things. Frings describes Scheler's views on the "functional existence of values," and writes: "Functional existence of something is at hand whenever this something must enter into a function with something else for it to become extant. A color, for instance, does not exist unless it is spread out on a surface. It exists in function with a surface that we see . . . values must enter into a function with something in order for them to be. By themselves, they are not objective entities. Hence, values are *independent* of objective things. The same holds for colors . . . Things like a cloth and a lawn are independent of 'green.' Both can be brown . . . Green does not care whether it is of the lawn or the cloth. A value like 'holy' likewise does not care whether it pertains to God, to a saint or a fetish. The independence that values have of things also has a negative aspect: it begets the possibility of deception in value experiences" (24). Or, we can say, it begets the possibility of destroying the value a thing has.

4 Relajo's double intentionality can also be thought of in terms of vertical and horizontal intentionality. The former is the directedness to objects in a straightforward way (vertically), while the latter has an intersubjective dimension, and implicates others around me in a *horizontal* and *a priori* way. Accordingly, horizontal intentionality involves an implicit reference to an already-existing intersubjectivity, or community, which is what relajo does (see Zahavi 1997).

5 See Sánchez (2012).

Chapter 2

1 In "The Nature of Mexica Ethics" (2019) James Maffie gives us an excellent etymological breakdown of the term. He writes: "The human-creator being relationship of mutual feeding and eating is captured by the semantic cluster of nepan-stem-constructed words of which nepantla is the best known. The processes designated by nepan-stem-constructed words include sexual intercourse, weaving, getting married, friendship, and reciprocal greeting, love, respect, and agreement. I call these nepantla-defined processes. Such processes are betwixt-and betweening, back-and-forthing, and mutually reciprocating, middling, and intermixing" (65).

2 Here, we can likewise translate "estamos nepantla" as "we are *being* nepantla," thereby highlighting its ontological aspect, an aspect that will prove increasingly significant as follows.

3 The rabbit is, of course, no stranger to Anglo-Western philosophy: Ludwig Wittgestein's "duck-rabbit" (Wittgesntein 1973) and W. V. O. Quine's (2013) "gavagai" are two of the most famous examples. The Mexica, however, had a less epistemological application for the rabbit-example.

4 Elsewhere, Uranga (2013) highlights nepantla's *ontological* priority and zozobra's emotive aspect: "This is nepantla. Not a 'synthesis,' but an 'oscillation,' to 'go from one end to another without rest.' The *mood* [*estado de animo*] that translates this *structure of being* is precisely zozobra.' In the *mood* of zozobra we do not know what to depend on, we vacillate between one and another 'law,' we are 'neutral,' 'in between,' 'nepantla'" (149). This should clarify the difference between nepantla and zozobra. Zozobra is a "mood," an emotive expression of nepantla, which is a "structure of being."

Nepantla is in this way a foundational aspect of our human beingness. To be human is to jump from place to place; it is not human to "synthesize," that is, to bundle our worlds, our experiences, and our identities into neat unities or easily identifiable "substances." What is human is to oscillate, to tirelessly go from one thing to another, from one experience to another, from the past to the future, or, if we are talking about specific cultural identities, from Mexican to American, without rest. Nepantla is what we are and what we *do*. When we *feel* it as mood, or as an "estado de animo," our nepantla is zozobra.

5   For more on this important Mexican philosopher, see Sanchez (2020).

Chapter 3

1   In Heidegger, for example, "[a]nxiety confronts Dasein with the knowledge that it is thrown into the world—always already delivered over to situations of choice and action which matter to it but which it did not itself fully choose or determine. It confronts Dasein with the determining and yet sheer contingent fact of its own worldly existence" (Mulhall 2005, 111).

2   Spanish Royal Academy, https://dle.rae.es/zozobra; elsewhere, http://etimologias.dechile.net/?zozobra.

3   Ortega y Gasset writes about "being conscious of living under the *zozobra* of an atrocious loss," pointing to zozobra as a state of disruption and unease (p. 479).

4   "Distress" is an uncommon translation of zozobra, but it does appear. See, for instance, Astor's *Nietzsche: La détresse du present* (2014), in which the French word "détresse" (distress, misery, anxiety) is translated into Spanish (Astor 2018) as "zozobra."

5   "Accidentality" and "being as accident" are described by Uranga in Part II of *Analysis.*

6   Although they are alike, zozobra and nepantla are not the same. My view notably differs from that of José Manuel Cuéllar Moreno (2018), Abraham Sapién (2021), and others who interpret zozobra and nepantla as identical in both structure and content. My characterization has it that nepantla is an ontological condition of existence while zozobra is an emotive

expression of that, a distinction that follows Uranga's (see footnote 26 of previous Chapter 2).

7   Ramón López Velarde, cited in Uranga (2021, 168).

Chapter 4

1   Thus, we find the phrase "the intimations of quantum mechanics," which refers to that world that quantum mechanics confidently posits as existing even without observable evidence (see Dorato 2015).

2   The term "transterrados" was used to describe intellectuals fleeing the Spanish Civil War of 1936. Most of these transterrados ended up in Mexico or other parts of South America. Bacca himself taught in Mexico City from 1942 to 1946.

3   And it is in Pascal that we find the famous dictum: "the heart has its reason that reason does not know of" (Pascal 2003, 79). Uranga was familiar with Pascal, confessing to the journalist Armando Ponce toward the end of his life: "I was educated in Christian schools by Christian brothers. I always loved to read Pascal, who for them was very dangerous" (Ponce 1988).

4   Of course, even for Pascal, lending privileged access to the heart does not equate to a demotion of reason. But reason's limits are evident in very obvious ways: reason, he says in Fragment 282 of the *Pensees*, cannot prove to us that we are dreaming; we just *know* it. But, this proves, against rationalist like Descartes and his ilk, "only the weakness of our reason . . . [and not] the uncertainty of all our knowledge" (Pascal 2003, 79). The heart, as source of knowledge, is thus less limited then reason in what it can and cannot "see." Ultimately, "It is the heart which experiences God, and not the reason. This, then, is faith: God felt by the heart, not by reason" (79).

5   Munch-Jurisic argues that disgust obscures moral judgment and is thus a destructive emotion.

6   According to this view: "The brain communicates to the viscera, including the gastrointestinal tract, through multiple parallel pathways, including the two branches of the autonomic nervous system (ANS), the hypothalamic–pituitary–adrenal (HPA) axis and the sympatho–adrenal axis (modulating the gut-associated lymphoid tissue), and descending monoaminergic

pathways (modulating gain of spinal reflexes and dorsal horn excitability)" (Mayer 2011).

7   To be fair, the kind of knowledge that Munch-Jurisic's attributes to gut feelings is the kind that would persuade or dissuade someone from committing a moral offense. But this greatly restricts the sort of knowledge one would get from gut feelings.

Chapter 5

1   There are issues of colonialism, imperialism, marginalization, and so on, that I will not get into here. There are also issues of appropriation of indigenous traditions that we should be attentive too; however, my purpose here is to showcase a variety of concepts for students of Mexican philosophy to think about, and I find the concept discussed in this chapter an original contribution to this project.

2   The Tojolab'al people are an original people living in various places of modern-day Chiapas, Mexico, Belize, Guatemala, and Honduras.

3   Throughout I assume that tik belongs in the Mexican philosophical tradition and, as such, that it goes a long way in explaining the idealizations with which we are familiar when it comes to Mexican sense of community.

4   Here Portilla anticipates something similar to what Crenshaw termed "intersectionality," although without the analytic flare that makes that concept so useful in feminist philosophy for contemporary analyses of oppression and power (see Crenshaw 2017).

5   The Lenkersdorf team heard "lalatik" and "tik" in almost every enunciation.

6   Lenkersdorf advocates the "Sapir–Whorf hypothesis," which holds that language or its structure affects the speakers thinking or worldview. I will not discuss this theory here.

Chapter 6

1   Pereda (1999) defines it in the following way: "by 'arrogant reason' I mean a way of believing, wishing, feeling, and acting [in which] the excesses

of the self are supported by an implacable disdain for the value of the
other and, in general, in thinking less of everything else. Furthermore . . .
whatever contempt there is for that which does not belong to the space
of one's own validation is systematically articulated and expressed" (14).
Or, as he later puts it: "The general presumptions governing arrogant
reasoning are supported by disdain and a rejection of any beliefs for which
they feel opposition or indifference" (2019b, 78).

2   Readers familiar with Gadamer, Fish, or the basic history of twentieth-
century philosophical hermeneutics will recognize the similarity between
Villoro's "figure of the world" and other concepts in that tradition. This is
not accidental, as Villoro was familiar with that tradition and, especially,
with Gadamer's *Truth and Method*. However, a comparative analysis of
these two figures is both beyond the scope of this chapter and, in my view,
detrimental to my purpose, which is to highlight the existence and value of
Mexican philosophy for the twenty-first century.

3   Twentieth-century Mexican philosophers that achieved international
recognition are few. The two that stand out are Leopoldo Zea and Luis
Villoro. These two also lived the longest, achieved such recognition
late in life, which perhaps suggests that had they not lived as long the
international community may have passed them over. Unlike some of their
peers, Zea and Villoro persevered and achieved what escaped Uranga,
Portilla, or Samuel Ramos. Such international recognition accounts for
Villoro's "Sahagún, or the Limits of the Discovery of the Other," a lecture
delivered *in English* in 1989 at the University of Maryland. This lecture
was published in 1992 by the University of Maryland in their Working
Papers series (Villoro 1992). The focus of this section is on this lecture.
However, I will read it in (and translate from) its Spanish version, which is
a translation from English to Spanish by Villoro himself and published in
1999 in *Estudios de la Cultural Nahuatl*, Vol. 29 (Villoro 1999). My reason
for settling on the Spanish version is simple and perhaps superficial:
although both versions articulate the problem of understanding inherent
in the encounter with the other, the Spanish is clearer that the English
about what I think is Villoro's most incisive contribution, namely, his
description of how a certain kind of arrogance kept the most distinguished
and learned Spanish missionaries from accepting the indigenous others in
their true difference.

Chapter 7

1 I've written about accidentality at length elsewhere (Sánchez 2021); see also Manuel Vargas' excellent analysis of the concept (Vargas 2021).

Bibliography

Alivrez, David and Frank D. Bean. 2001. "The Mexican American Family," in *Interdisciplinary Perspectives on the New Immigration, Vol. 4: The New Immigrant and American Family*, edited by Marcelo M. Suárez-Orozco, Carola Suárez-Orozco, and Desirée Qin-Hilliard, 219–40. New York: Routledge.

Antony, Luise M. 2016. "Bias: Friend or Foe? Reflections on Saulish Skepticism," in *Implicit Bias and Philosophy, Volume I*, edited by Michael Brownstein and Jennifer Saul, 157–90. Oxford: Oxford University Press.

Antuna, Marcos. 2018. "What We Talk About When We Talk About Nepantla: Gloria Anzaudua and the Queer Fruit of Aztec Philosophy," *Journal of Latinos and Education* 17, no. 2: 159–63.

Anzaldúa, Gloria. 1987. *Borderlands/La Frontera: La New Mestiza*. San Francisco: Aunt Lute Books.

Anzaldúa, Gloria. 2009. *The Gloria Anzaldua Reader*, edited by AnaLouise Keating. Durham: Duke University Press.

Astor, Dorian. 2018. *Nietzsche: La zozobra del presente*, translated by Jordi Bayod Brau. Madrid: Acantilado. In French: 2014. *Nietzsche: La détresse du present*. Paris: Gallimard.

Bacca, Juan David Garcia. 1991. *Sobre el Quijote y Don Quijote de La Mancha: Ejercicios literario-filosoficos*. Barcelona: Anthropos.

Bacca, Juan David Garcia. 2003. *Introducción literaria a la filosofía*. Navarra, Spain: Anthropos.

Becker, Ernest. 1973. *The Denial of Death*. New York: The Free Press.

Bergson, Henri. 1912. *An Introduction to Metaphysics*, translated by T. E. Hulme. New York: G.P. Putnam's Sons.

Bolom Pale, Manuel. 2019. *Chanubtasel-p'ijubtasel: Reflexiones filosóficas de los pueblos originarios*. Mexico: CLACSO.

Bondy, Augusto Salazar. 1968. *Existe una filosofia en nuestra America?* Madrid: Siglo XXI Editores España.

Buber, Martin. 1986. *I and Thou*, translated by Ronald Gregory. New York: Charles Scribner's Son.

Castellano, Rosario. 2017. "On Feminine Culture," in *Mexican Philosophy in the 20th Century: Essential Readings*, edited by Carlos Alberto Sánchez and Robert Eli Sanchez Jr., 206–15. New York: Oxford University Press.

Clayton, Ashley B., Mary C. Medina, and Angela Wiseman. 2019. "Culture and Community: Perspectives from First-Year, First-Generation-in-College Latino Students," *Journal of Latinos and Education* 18, no. 2: 134–50.

Cooper, William F. 2010. "Normal Philosophy," in *A Companion to Latin American Philosophy*, edited by Susana Nuccetelli, Otavio Bueno, and Ofelia Schutte, 128–41. Malden: Wiley-Blackwell Publishing.

Crenshaw, Kimberlé W. 2017. *On Intersectionality: Essential Writings*. New York: The New Press.

Cotkin, George. 2005. *Existential America*. Baltimore: John Hopkins University Press.

Cuéllar Moreno, José Manuel. 2018. *La revolución inconclusa: la filosofía de Emilio Uranga, artifice oculto del PRI*. México DF: Ariel.

Cusicanqui, Silvia Rivera. 2018. *Un mudo ch'ixi es posible. Ensayos desde un presente en crisis*. Buenos Aires: Tinta Limón.

Diaz-Guerrero, Ruben. 1975. *Psychology of the Mexican: Culture and Personality*. Austin: The University of Texas Press.

Dorato, Mauro. 2015. "Events and the Ontology of Quantum Mechanics," *Topoi* 34, no. 2: 369–78.

Durán, Diego. 1994. *History of the Indies of New Spain*, translated by Doris Heyden. Norman: University of Oklahoma Press.

Emerson, Ralph Waldo. 1993. *Self-Reliance and Other Essays*. New York: Dover Publications.

Fanon, Franz. 2004. *The Wretched of the Earth*, translated by Richard Philcox. New York: Grove/Atlantic.

Freud, Sigmund. 1950. *Beyond the Pleasure Principle*, translated by J. Strachey. New York: Hogarth Press.

Frings, Manfred. 1997. *The Mind of Max Scheler: The First Comprehensive Guide Based on the Complete Works*. Milwaukee: Marquette University Press.

Frost, Elsa Cecilia. 1972. *Las categorías de la cultura mexicana*. México: UNAM.

Frost, Elsa Cecilia. 2018. "Acerca de Nepantla," published online, August 27, 2018, http://www.academia.org.mx/noticias/item/acerca-de-nepantla-por -elsa-cecilia-frost.

Gracia, Jorge. 2003. "Ethnic Labels in Philosophy: The Case of Latin American Philosophy," in *Latin American Philosophy: Issues, Currents, Debates*, edited by Eduardo Mendieta, 57–67. Bloomington: Indiana University Press.

Gracia, Jorge and Manuel Vargas. 2018. "Latin American Philosophy," *The Stanford Encyclopedia of Philosophy*, edited by Edward N. Zalta, https://plato.stanford.edu/archives/sum2018/entries/latin-american-philosophy/

Guerra, Ricardo. 1948. "Jean Paul Sartre, filosofo de la libertad," *Filosofía y Letras* 16, no. 32: 295–307.

Heidegger, Martin. 1962. *Being and Time*, translated by John McQuarrie and Edward Robinson. New York: Harper and Row.

Heidegger, Martin. 1998. "Letter on Humanism," in *Pathmarks*, edited by William McNeill. Cambridge: Cambridge University Press.

Hierro, Graciela. 1981. "La filosofía de Rosario Castellanos," *Plural* 10, no. 120: 29–33.

Hurtado, Guillermo (ed.). 2006. *El Hiperión*. Mexico: Universidad Nacional Autonoma de Mexico.

Hurtado, Guillermo (ed.). 2007. *El Búho y la Serpiente: Ensayos sobre la filosofía en México en el siglo XX*. México: Universidad Nacional Autónoma de México.

Hurtado, Guillermo (ed.). 2021. "Filosofia Mexicana y Mexican Philosophy," *La razón*, August 28, 2021, https://www.razon.com.mx/opinion/columnas/guillermo-hurtado/filosofia-mexicana-mexican-philosophy-449080

Husserl, Edmund. 1960. *Cartesian Meditations*, translated by Dorion Cairns. The Hague: Martinus Nijhoff.

Husserl, Edmund. 1983. *Ideas Pertaining to a Pure Phenomenology and to a Phenomenological Philosophy, First Book*, translated by F. Kersten. Dordrecht: Kluwer Academic Publishers.

Husserl, Edmund. 2001. *Logical Investigations, Volume II*, translated by Dermot Moran. London: Routledge.

James, William. 1890. The Principles of Psychology. New York: Henry Holt.

Kant, Immanuel. 1999. *Critique of Pure Reason*, translated by Paul Guyer and Allen Wood. Cambridge: Cambridge University Press.

Kant, Immanuel. 2012. *Groundwork for the Metaphysics of Morals*, translated by Mary Gregor. Cambridge: Cambridge University Press.

Kauffman, Walter. 1975. *Existentialism from Dostoevsky to Sartre*. New York: Penguin.

Keating, AnaLouise. 2006. "From Borderlands and New Mestizas to Nepantlas and Nepantleras," *Human Architecture: Journal of the Sociology of Self-Knowledge* Iv, Special Issue: 5–16.

Kelly, Sean D. 2002. "Merleau-Ponty on the Body," *Ratio* 15: 376–91.

Kierkegaard, Søren. 1981. *The Concept of Anxiety: A Simple Psychologically Orienting Deliberation on the Dogmatic Issue of Hereditary Sin*, translated by Reidar Thmote. Princeton: Princeton University Press.

Kirloskar-Steinbach, Monika and Leah Kalmanson. 2021. *A Practical Guide to World Philosophies*. London. Bloomsbury.

Lenkersdorf, Carlos. 2005. *Filosofía en clave tojolabal*. Mexico: Porrúa.

Levinas, Emmanuel. 1991. *Totality and Infinity*, translated by Alphonso Lingis. Dordrecht: Kluwer Academic Publishers.

Maffie, James. 2015. *Aztec Philosophy: Understanding a World in Motion*. Boulder: University of Colorado Press.

Maffie, James. 2019. "The Nature of Mexica Ethics," in *Comparative Metaethics*, edited by James Maffie, 60–80. New York: Routledge.

Mayer, Emeran A. 2011. "Gut Feelings: The Emerging Biology of Gut-Brain Communication," *Nature Review of Neuroscience* 12, no. 8. Online: https://doi.org/10.1038/nrn3071

Mckee Irwin, Robert. 2017. "Solitude," in *Modern Mexican Culture*, edited by Stuart Day, 148–65. Tucson: Univesrity of Arizona Press.

Mulhall, Stephen. 2005. *Heidegger and Being and Time*. New York: Routledge.

Munch-Jurisic, Ditte Marie. 2018. "Perpetrator Disgust: A Morally Destructive Emotion," in *Emotions and Mass Atrocities: Philosophical and Theoretical Explorations*, edited by Thomas Brudholm and Johannes Lang, 142–61. London: Cambridge University Press.

Munch-Jurisic, Ditte Marie. 2022a. *Perpetrator Disgust: The Moral Limits of Gut Feelings*. London: Oxford University Press.

Munch-Jurisic, Ditte Marie. 2020b. "The Right to Feel Comfortable: Implicit Bias and the Moral Potential of Discomfort," *Ethical Theory and Moral Practice* 23, no. 1: 237–50.

Natanson, Maurice. 1952. "Jean-Paul Sartre's Philosophy of Freedom," *Social Research* 19, no. 3: 364–80.

Ortega y Gasset, José. 2000. *Mediations on Quixote*, translated by Evelyn Rugg and Diego Marin. Champaign: University of Illinois Press.

Ortega y Gasset, José. 2009. *La razon historica. Obras Completas IX*. Madrid: Taurus.

Pascal, Blaise. 2003. *Pensées*, translated by W. F. Trotter. New York: Dover Publications.

Paz, Octavio. 1985. *The Labyrinth of Solitude*, translated by Lysander Kemp. New York: Grove Press.

Penn, Julia M. *Linguistic Relativity versus Innate Ideas: The Origins of the Sapir-Whorf Hypothesis in German Thought*. The Hague: Mouton.

Pereda, Carlos. 1999. *Critica de la razón arrogante*. Cuatro panfletos civiles. Mexico: Taurus.

Pereda, Carlos. 2013. *La filosofia en Mexico en el siglo XX: Apuntes de un participante*. Mexico: Direccion General de Publicaciones.

Pereda, Carlos. 2019a. "On Mexican Philosophy, For Example," *Comparative Philosophy* 10, no. 1: 192–207.

Pereda, Carlos. 2019b. *Lessons in Exile*, translated by Sean Manning. London: Brill/Rodopi.

Pereda, Carlos. 2020. *Libertad: Un panfleto civil*. Mexico: Universidad Nacional de Mexico.

Pereda, Carlos. 2021. *Pensar a Mexico: entre otros reclamos*. Mexico: Gedisa.

Plato. 2007. *The Republic*, translated by Desmond Lee. New York: Penguin Classics.

Ponce, Armando. 1988. "La filosofía del mexicano ya no tiene sentido: Emilio Uranga," *Processo*, no. 627: 48–50.

Portilla, Jorge. 2012. "Phenomenology of Relajo," translated by Carlos Alberto Sánchez, in *The Suspension of Seriousness: On the Phenomenology of Jorge Portilla*, 123–200. Albany: State University of New York Press

Portilla, Jorge. 2017. "Community, Greatness, and Misery in Mexican Life," translated by Carlos Alberto Sánchez, in *Mexican Philosophy in the 20th Century: Essential Readings*, edited by Carlos Alberto Sánchez and Robert Eli Sanchez, 178–95. New York: Oxford University Press.

Quijano, Anibal. 2000. "Coloniality of Power, Eurocentrism, and Latin America," *Nepantla: Views from the South* 1, no. 3: 533–80.

Quine, W. V. O. 2013. *Word and Object*. Cambridge, MA: The MIT Press.

Ramos, Samuel. 1962. *Profile of Man and Culture in Mexico*, translated by Peter G. Earle. Austin: University of Texas Press.

Reuter, Martina. 1999. "Merleau-Ponty's Notion of Pre-Reflective Intentionality," *Synthese* 118: 69–88.

Romanell, Patrick. 1952. *Making of the Mexican Mind: A Study in Recent Mexican Thought*. Lincoln: University of Nebraska Press.

Romero, Francisco. 1943. "Tendencias Contemporáneas en el Pensamineto Hispanoamericano," *Philosophy and Phenomenological Research* 4, no. 2: 127–34.

Rorty, Richard. 2006. *Take Care of Freedom and Truth Will Take Care of Itself*, edited by Eduardo Mendieta. Palo Alto: Stanford University Press.

Sánchez, Carlos Alberto. 2012. *The Suspension of Seriousness: On the Phenomenology of Jorge Portilla*. Albany: State University of New York Press.

Sánchez, Carlos Alberto. 2013. "Death and the Colonial Difference," *Journal of the Philosophy of Life* 3, no. 3: 168–89.

Sánchez, Carlos Alberto. 2016. *Contingency and Commitment: Mexican Existentialism and the Place of Philosophy*. Albany: State University of New York Press.

Sánchez, Carlos Alberto. 2019a. "Authenticity and the Right to Philosophy: On Latin American Philosophy's Great Debate," in *The Cambridge History of Philosophy, 1945–2015*, edited by Kelly Becker and Iain D. Thomson, 679–91. Cambridge: Cambridge University Press.

Sánchez, Carlos Alberto. 2019b. "(M)existentialism," *The Philosophers Magazine*, March 3, 2019. https://www.philosophersmag.com/essays/197 -m-existentialism

Sánchez, Carlos Alberto. 2020. "Elsa Cecilia Frost: Culture and Nepantla," *Newsletter for Hispanic/Latino Issues in Philosophy* 20, no. 1: 5–9.

Sapién, Abraham. Forthcoming. "Zozobra: Somos humanos y nos llaman mexicanos," *Los procesos corpoemocionales en los estudios de género y sexualidades, Vol. VII*. Facultad de Estudios Superiores Iztacala UNAM y Universidad Jesuita de Guadalajara ITESO.

Sánchez, Carlos Alberto. 2021. "*Critical Introduction*," to Emilio Uranga's Analysis of Mexican Being. New York Bloomsbury, 1–89.

Sartre, Jean-Paul. 1992. *Being and Nothingness*, translated by Hazel Barnes. Washington Square Press.

Sartre, Jean-Paul. 2005. *Nausea*, translated by Lloyd Alexander. New York: New Directions.

Sartre, Jean-Paul. 2006. *Critique of Dialectical Reason*, translated by Quintin Hoare. London: Verso.

Solomon, Robert. 2004. *Existentialism*. Oxford: Oxford University Press.

Stinchcombe, Arthur. 1986. "Reason and Rationality," *Sociological Theory* 4, no. 2: 151–66.

Sy, Susan R. and Jessica Romero. 2008. "Family Responsibilities among Latina College Students From Immigrant Families," *Journal of Hispanic Higher Education* 7, no. 3: 212–27.

Tarm, Michael and Jacques Billeaud. 2021. "The Mob made Me Do It: Rioters Claim," *AP News*, May 23. Download May 27, 2021. https://apnews.com/article/dc-wire-michael-pence-donald-trump-capitol-siege-government-and-politics-6434e5ba1e5d762be91dc971706dd0b9

Thouvenot, Marc. 2014. *Diccionario náhuatl-español basado en los diccionarios de Alonso de Molina con el náhuatl normalizado.* México: Universidad Nacional Autónoma de México, Instituto de Investigaciones Históricas.

Troncoso Pérez, Ramón. 2011. "Nepantla, una aproximación al término," in *Tierras prometidas. De la colonia a la independencia*, edited by Bernat Castany, Bernat Hernandez, Guillermo Seres, and Mercedes Serna, 375–98. Barcelona: Centro para la Edición de los Clásicos Españoles-UAB.

Uranga, Emilio. 1948. "Maurice Merleau-Ponty: Fenomenología y existencialismo," *Filosofía y Letras* 30: 233–49.

Uranga, Emilio. 1949. "Dialogo con Maurice Merleau-Ponty," *Mexico en la cultura* (March 13): 9–10.

Uranga, Emilio. 1951. "Notas para un estudio del mexicano," *Cuadernos Americanos*, no. 3: 114–28.

Uranga, Emilio. 2013. *Analisis del ser del mexicano y otros escritos sobre la filosofía de lo mexicano (1949–1952).* Edited by Guillermo Hurtado. México: Bonilla Artigas Editores.

Uranga, Emilio. 2017. "Essay on an Ontology of the Mexican," translated by Carlos Alberto Sánchez, in *Mexican Philosophy in the 20th Century: Essential Readings*, edited by Carlos Alberto Sánchez and Robert E. Sanchez, 168–77. New York: Oxford University Press.

Uranga, Emilio. 2021. *Analysis of Mexican Being*, translated by Carlos Alberto Sánchez. London: Bloomsbury.

Van Norden, Brian W. 2022. "Readings on Less Commonly Taught Philosophies (LCTP)," *Multicultural Philosophy*. http://www.bryanvannorden.com/suggestions-for-further-reading.

Vargas, Manuel. 2021. "The Philosophy of Accidentality," *Journal of the American Philosophical Association* 6, no. 4: 391–409.

Velarde, Ramón López. 1919. *Zozobra.* México: Ediciones México Moderno.

Velazquez, Mariano. 2005. *The New Velazquez Spanish and English Dictionary.* El Monte: Academic Learning Company.

Villalobos, Raul Trejo and Obed Frausto. 2019. *Filosofia de los pueblos originarios*. San Cristobal: Universidad Autónoma de Chiapas.

Villegas, Abelardo. 1979. *La filosofia de lo mexicano*. México: Universidad Nacional Autónoma de México.

Villegas, Abelardo. 1992. "Polémica de las mafias," *Proceso*, no. 798: February 17, 1992.

Villoro, Luis. 1949. "Genesis y proyecto del existencialismo en Mexico," *Filosofia y letras* 18, no. 36: 233–44.

Villoro, Luis. 1975. "Lo indecible en el Tractatus," *Critica* 7, no. 19: 5–39.

Villoro, Luis. 1992. "Sahagún or the Limits of the Discover of the Other," in *Working Papers no. 2*, 3–16. College Park: University of Maryland.

Villoro, Luis. 1998. *Belief, Personal, and Propositional Knowledge*. Translated by Ernest Sosa and Douglas McDermid. Boston: Brill Rodopi.

Villoro, Luis. 1999. "Sahagún o los limites del descubrimiento del otro," *Estudios de la Cultura Nahuatl* 29: 15–26.

Villoro, Luis. 2017. "Solitude and Communion," translated by Minerva Ahumada, in *Mexican Philosophy in the 20th Century: Essential Readings*, edited by Carlos Alberto Sánchez and Robert Eli Sanchez, 141–55. Oxford: Oxford University Press.

Wild, John. 1960. "Existentialism as a Philosophy," *The Journal of Philosophy* 57, no. 2: 45–62.

Winget, J. R. and E. S. Park. 2022. "Discharged in D.C.: The Role of Disinhibition in the Behavior of Insurrection Group Members," *Group Dynamics: Theory, Research, and Practice*. Advance online publication. https://doi.org/10.1037/gdn0000182

Wittgenstein, Ludwig. 1973. *Philosophical Investigations*. Translated by G. E. M. Anscombe. New York: Prentice Hall.

Zahavi, Dan. 1997. "Horizontal Intentionality and Transcendental Intersubjectivity," *Tijdschrift Voor Filosofie* 59, no. 2: 304–21.

Zea, Leopoldo. 1942. "En torno a una filosofía Americana," *Cuadernos Americanos* 1, no. 3: 63–78.

Zea, Leopoldo. 1949. "El existencialismo como filosofia de la responsabilidad," *El Nacional*, June 5, 1949, section 3.

Zea, Leopoldo. 1992. *The Role of the Americas in History*. Translated by Sonja Karsen. Savage: Rowman & LIttlefield Publishers.

Zea, Leopoldo. 2017. "Philosophy as Commitment," translated by Amy Oliver, in *Mexican Philosophy in the 20th Century: Essential Readings*, edited by Carlos Alberto Sánchez and Robert Eli Sanchez, 125–40. Oxford: Oxford University Press.

Index